"Some of the best advise I've read for anyone wanting to break away from conventional career methods"
 —Dan Waldorf, Vice President Surety
  Alexander & Alexander

"*Landing on Your Feet* sends a message to anyone that has wanted to do their own thing. The philosophy Mr. Waldorf outlines has obviously worked well for him."
 —Scott Gidley, MBA
  The Equitable

"Mr. Waldorf is the consumate entrepreneur. He has carefully extracted success principles that have contributed to his success and made them understandable."
 —Jerry Stokes, Publisher
  Todays Pawnbroker magazine

LANDING ON YOUR FEET

By
James Waldorf

All rights reserved.
Copyright 1992 by James Waldorf
This book may not be reproduced in
whole or in part without permission.
For information contact James Waldorf
Sales/Publications
P.O. Box 399
Yucaipa, CA 92399

ISBN 0-9635497-0-7

CONTENTS

Dedication vii

Acknowledgements ix

Forward xiii

1 Thank God I've Lost My Job 1
2 The Flame That Turned into an Inferno 7
3 The Game Plan 15
4 Applying the Mastermind Alliance 23
5 The Positive Attitude: Get it, Keep it, Use it! 29
6 Isn't it Great Being Here at the Bottom 51
7 Why Do You Want All That Money? 65
8 Entrepreneurial Examples to Relate To 75
9 Getting Back to Basics: Small is Better 123
10 The Heart-Mind Relationship 133
11 The Difference Between a Job and a Career 141
12 Knowing Your Limits 151
13 Entrepreneurial Opportunities 159

DEDICATION

This book is dedicated to my father in law Robert (Mac) McDougal. Mac passed away this year after a long battle with an illness he was confronted with less than a year after he retired, at age 60. Mac raised a large family of 6 children, and passed along all of the best moral values and work ethic that anyone could hope to have. He was a great role model as a family man, and was respected and loved by all those he knew. He was taken advantage of by too many, that knew he would give them the shirt off his back, and he did. He died with the dignity of being loved and respected, but not being able to pay for his funeral. He deserved more I believe, after devoting 37 years of his life, working sometimes 15 hours a day, for a fortune 500 company (one of the 500 largest U.S. companies). Upon his death his widow ceased to receive any pension benefits at all from the same company he dedicated his life to. I believe that my friend Mac saw in his later years, that hard work and long hours alone, given to an entity other than your own, was not the answer. But in those later years it was simply too late to go back to middle age, and review his perception of security. And as most Americans, his blind faith was placed in the idea that working for a very big secure company meant that someday he would be looked after by that company. Just as he had looked after that company's best interests for 37 years. To the disappointment of my friend Mac, and a lot of others, job security has turned out to be the biggest myth in America today.

I am sorry that I could not have compiled the survival philosophy outlined in my book early enough to have benefited Mac. But hopefully you will gain something from it, and perhaps learn how to land on your feet, inspite of the uncontrollable events in your own life.

ACKNOWLEDGEMENTS

The people that really deserve credit for making this book possible are those entrepreneurs whose successes, and failures, became my teachers, and I their student.

Mr. Steve Young, my true best friend, who allowed me to watch closely as he built a recycling business from scratch, into a 200 million dollar a year privately owned enterprise, probably the largest of its kind in the western hemisphere.

The three brothers and their father, that in 1983 placed their faith in me when I became unemployed, by allowing me the exclusive rights to sell their American built machinery, that they so diligently developed to compete head to head with their much larger Japanese competitors. And who, by 1989, Business Week Magazine acknowledged as capturing 80% of the domestic machining center businesses in their respective fields. And who is today producing over 100 machines a month, 98 more than in 1983. Francis, Adrian, David, and Larry (FADAL) DeCaussin gave me their trust and friendship, as well as total faith philosophy to negotiate whatever it took to get a deal done. These dedicated gentlemen, and their families are the closest examples of true unlimited success principles as applied to the machine tool business in modern times.

Mr. Tony Maglica, owner of the world famous Mag Lite flashlight company, for his pursuit and capture of the quality flashlight market that I attempted to pursue before I was truly ready for success. Mr. Maglica provided me with a concise realism of my shortcomings in manufacturing that had ultimately contributed to my failure.

My current business partner, Mr. Errol Brown, for possessing what I had lacked in manufacturing expertise, when I decided after 15 years to roll the dice and attempt to manufacture a product once again. Errol brought to the table of our firearms manufacturing company, the patience and discipline in manufacturing, as well as faith in my ability to achieve the goal I envisioned for almost 20 years.

My long time mentor, Mr. Napoleon Hill, who called my attention to the mastermind alliance principle, in his publication of *Think And Grow Rich*. Of which to this day I still carry the copy that I had purchased in 1974, dog eared and highlighted, it is one of my most valued belongings. His writings had a profound influence on my life.

To the ladies that assisted in critiqueing my writing of *Landing On Your Own Feet*. My wife Karen, who had a hard time with the initial scribbled version and patiently read and suggested. Mrs. Ruby Simmpson, herself an entrepreneur, who called to my attention the real problems facing real life would be entrepreneurial women that are faced with certain special problems. Susan Mathews whose bright shining new degree in psychology from the University of Wisconsin was tested in evaluating the psychological value of the book to the people that will be reading it.

Jennifer Simpson whose own success at a young age of 17 in publishing her 4 year old music

ACKNOWLEDGEMENTS

journal won my admiration quickly as being a true life example of the achievement philosopy not recognizing age as a barrier. And who diligently prodded through my misspelling and unpunctuated literary disaster, and asked are you sure you want to be an author? Jennifer made many suggestions not all of which I followed, but had I, this book would have been absolutely perfect.

    Mr. John Reiss whose imagination enabled him to take a character idea and bring him to life as the little fellow landing on his feet on the runway of life, as illustrated on the book's cover. John also saw in each chapter's title heading a character that best illustrated that chapter. I hope you enjoy these little guys that so dutifully convey the contents of each chapter.

FORWARD

Have you ever wanted something very very badly and thought that it was out of your reach? Or have you ever thought that you could achieve a much higher degree of success, but for reasons that you don't control you simply stopped trying? Then join with me in exploring the career paths of everyday people that grasped the entrepreneurial opportunities that they sought and turned them into furtunes, or at minimum exceptionally good incomes.

I hope that by exploring the entrepreneurial path with me, you will see first hand a step by step formula that will put you at far better odds of assuring your success. You will come away with, I hope, an enlightened sense of who you are, and the limitless capabilities that everyone in the world has the potential of developing and capatalizing on. And above all, YOU will become the master of your own destiny without allowing others to pull your strings.

It is obvious that corporate America has made some major mistakes during the past decade. Corporate America will undoubtedly place the blame on government, and they rightfully should to a large degree. But what happens to those of us that are caught in this paradox of ineptness of these decision makers that most Americans had trusted their careers to only to be disappointed by either unemployment or underemployment status? Why is most of America a two income family that allows very little time to develop the growth of their children because they are too busy scratching to make ends meet?

At this writing it is estimated that national unemployment is 8%, around 11% in California, and much higher in select cities. I don't think you have to be a genius to see that these statistics are very conservative when you consider those that have quit receiving unemployment benefits. When these are considered, true unemployment could be around 20%. With these numbers, and the numbers of Americans that are UNDER EMPLOYED, and earning far less than they are truly worth, total combinations of the two are more than likely 50% of the entire country's work force.

The purpose of my book is to educate the large numbers of people that have fallen into the above categories. The philosophy in this book works. Whether or not you, the reader, choose to apply the principles and move on to bigger and better things, as you will discover, is entirely up to you. Inspiration in writing this book was derived from my own failures at achieving the elusive success formula, that I knew was out there to be found. Now that I've found it, I'd like to share it with as many limitless thinking people who would like to learn, and possibly benefit from it as well.

My credentials are best given in the title, due to the tremendous amount of runway I used in Landing on My Feet. Not everyone reading my book will take the plunge. Not everyone has possibly seen himself in some part of this writing, as the person that was victim of events out of their control. I am happy for those that are happy with their status at their current endeavors. I am curious though, to see at what particular point in their lives they will identify with the thoughts contained in my book.

It is unlikely that a large percentage of those currently underemployed will abandon their jobs and seek out their true worth via entrepreneurial paths. This simple law of nature will give those of us willing to take some risk, the very best odds for our success.

THANK GOD I'VE LOST MY JOB

1

What a blessing this situation would turn out to be, although during that period of my life I remember viewing it as most people naturally would, as a devastation.

My two daughters were ten and fourteen years old. I had a mortgage that amounted to about sixty percent of my modest home's value, a savings account with about five thousand dollars in it, a car payment, and other obligations. My wife did not work. This was the dismal picture that was painted for me in 1982, when the recession had hit the capital equipment market. I was given my walking notice by the Fortune 500 company that I had worked for as Western Regional Sales Manager. During the same period my seemingly safe, secure "big company" had relieved fifteen thousand others of their positions as well.

It is amazing how important that $2800 was, especially since my debt load and monthly expenses totalled almost all of that. This I later identified as one of my major thinking problems, and one that

almost everyone reading this book may have as well.
If you have not yet identified the "major thinking problem" that I am talking about, I will help you out. My comfort zone was too low. "What is a comfort zone?" you may ask. Well, that is what I have come to refer to as the amount of income with which you are satisfied.
Everyone's comfort zone is directly indexed to his or her lifestyle. In my case I was happy having a monthly surplus of perhaps three hundred dollars, perhaps half of which would have been spent on entertainment, and half of which would have been saved. Well, you don't have to be a genius to see that the discipline I had was not going to make me rich. We will touch on that discipline in a later chapter because that is a topic in itself and a key ingredient in implementing your plan.
Little did I know that the path that I would take over the next few years would turn my life around entirely, from my dismal outlook back in 1982 when I had officially joined the ranks of the unemployed and had unkowingly for my entire working career been underemployed.
Since I've always disliked hearing writers and philosophers refer too much to their own successes and not enough to their failures, I shall attempt to highlight my own failures and use my successes only as examples when there is an important lesson to be extracted from the example. I would like to mention now, though, that my first year's income as a result of being forced into entrepreneurship was $100,000. Within four years I had achieved

millionaire status, meaning that my assets exceeded my liabilities by over one million dollars. My income exceeded two hundred and fifty thousand dollars that year. This year marks my tenth year as an independent entrepreneur. I expect to earn as income between $1,200,000 and two million dollars. My current net worth is between $3,000,000 and $4,500,000. These figures are not bogus, overstated real estate values but are tangible liquid estimates. This is the only mention in the book of how well I have done. After all, you have invested in my book to learn how to achieve for yourself.

LANDING ON YOUR FEET

THE FLAME THAT TURNED INTO AN INFERNO

THE FLAME THAT TURNED INTO AN INFERNO

2

In this chapter I will discuss motivation. What motivates one person may not necessarily motivate another. What is important to one person may not be very important to another.

A good example of this can be examined by asking someone that you know that is at a modest economic level of living how important it is for him or her to become rich. One person may respond by saying, "You know, it is really not that important to me. I get along okay, enjoy recreational activities like skiing and fishing, and I'm comfortable where I am in life." Let's evaluate this person for a minute. How old is he? What are his incentives to achieve more?

Perhaps he is truly satisfied where he is economically. After all, he does take time to go skiing and fishing. What every person has in common with others is that each has twenty-four hours in a day, no more, no less. What one person does with his twenty-four hours and another with his can be, and generally is, entirely different, depending only on his priorities in life. Therefore it may be entirely wrong to judge a person's "successes" only on his economic well-being. When most people refer to success, though, it is generally interpreted as money. This popular misconception is the furthest thing from the truth.

In the mind of the person mentioned above, he is successful. He has achieved what he wanted to achieve, although perhaps not economically. He gets to go skiing and fishing quite often, and he had identified that as his priority and has achieved that goal; therefore, he is successful.

Now let us use the same example person above. Let us assume that he had just received the same bad news that I received in 1982. What now?

Let us assume that he was like me and had about five thousand dollars in the bank and had the same monthly expenses. This means that he can continue his lifestyle uninterrupted for about two months with no sacrifices at all. Well, what happens after two months? Frightening, isn't it? Especially when he may have assumed that he would surely find work within two months.

The philosophy that is important to recognize here is that taking something for granted is a very bad method of operation, and making assumptions could put you in a perilous situation. You can and do control your own destiny by your own actions. There is no such thing as luck!

Your actions and planning will mean the difference between your success or failure. Although you can control most of your actions, no one is ever totally in control of anything. There will always be variables that are out of your control. Recognize those variables and get on top of them if you can, if they are detrimental to your plan. If not, put them out of your mind. Using the same example person, let us now see why he is so vulnerable. For one thing, like almost every one of us, he worked for someone. This fact alone indicates that he never had any control over his destiny. Never has this been more painfully apparent than during the early part of this decade, when a lot of well-paid banking VPs and presidents, as well as savings and loan executives, aerospace managers, insurance executives, and nearly all basic industry executives, with very few exceptions, i.e. medical professionals, were confronted with the shocking horror of being out of work and without income.

After seeing people who have been put out to pasture without cause, and not as a reflection of their professional ability, it is very clear that no one is immune to job loss. However, the way that one person handles it may be very different indeed from the way another person may handle it, and probably the single most important thing to recognize is that there are twenty-four hours in a day, no more, no less. Also realize that, by planning each day's time usage, you can most likely eliminate the bad aspects associated with being unemployed. Keep in mind that if you recognize the importance of good time management early on, you will be way ahead of the game and on your way to your future successes in whatever profession you choose. Later in the book we will see some direct examples of many people who have prospered by employing good time utilization.

Our economic example in this chapter shows that our man had a comfort zone that was too low, certainly a lot lower than mine, although he probably got to go fishing and skiing a lot more than I did when I was in his shoes. To that end he was successful. On the other hand, by continuing his lifestyle priorities for two months after becoming unemployed he would be out of luck! However, if at the first sign of bad news he had dug in and utilized his time wisely to produce income or devise his plan to do so, he would be back on track in the very near future.

THINGS TO REMEMBER
Time utilization
You no longer work from 8:00 to 5:00.
You may find it necessary to devote twenty hours a day, but not forever.
Recognize and place in priority a game plan that equals income.
The one basic human motivator that some claim to be the most powerful human motivator that exists is sex. For that matter, sex could quite possibly be the most prevalent motivator of all life forms. Take the example of the young man interested in dating the lady of his fancy. His pursuit in the direction of receiving her affection is relentless. The mental energy expended during his pursuit is enormous. During the pursuit she occupies most of his thought process leading to the eventual sexual encounter.

Have you ever driven down the street and seen a couple of dogs doing it right in the middle of the road, totally oblivious to the traffic swerving to avoid them? I recall that, when I was a child, our neighbors' dog and our dog did it right through a chain-link fence. What determination! It is a perfect example of the motivational thought process through to the accomplishment of the goal.

How often have you seen a young man's grades suffering in school, failing because his concentrated effort was too far below his belt? We refer to this a lot as a guy who thinks with the wrong part of his anatomy, but it is absolutely true! How about the guy that is failing in business or at his profession because he is spending his thought energy on his latest heartthrob?

How often are a man's failures blamed on a woman, or vice versa? Not often enough are man's successes attributed to a woman, however, and it is worth noting that most very successful men have ladies who are motivating them.

Imagine the power that you would possess in your pursuit of entrepreneurship if you were able to channel proportionately the strongest human motivational force of the universe into the direction of personal achievement in business or any other field. Simply put, by applying the same proportionate amount of energy that would be expended in the pursuit of mating to the achievement of another goal, your likelihood of success will be achieved soon.

14 THE FLAME THAT TURNED INTO AN INFERNO

THE GAME PLAN

3

Anyone who has participated in team sports, watched team sports, begun a business, planned a family vacation, or even gone on a shopping trip has had to devise a plan. Planning can go from what you plan to watch on television tonight to what you plan on investing in in the future. Everything that we do requires some amount of planning.

A guy starts a new business, works at it diligently, uses his twenty-four hour day very well, but he fails. Is this a sad story? You better believe it is. But is it that uncommon? Not at all. Unfortunately the ranks of the unemployed are not the only thing that is on the rise; business failures are on the climb as well.

So what happens after his failure? It entirely depends on the person. His failure was a direct reflection of his planning, or lack of planning. What is unfortunate about any business failure is that the entrepreneur will now have his thought process cluttered with negative thoughts about being his own person in business. Quite often the entrepreneur is psychologically devastated. It is also unfortunate that the psychological effect will probably stay with him for a while, possibly preventing him from ever trying his hand at business again and will convince him to bow to the pressure and do the unthinkable thing: find a job.

Looking at the above example, there is no shame in a failure of anything in life. In the above example the entrepreneur gave one hundred percent, used his time wisely, did everything right. Why wasn't he successful? Let's back up to the previous chapter and reflect on things that may have been out of his control which obviously he could not change because he did not even recognize them. He did not recognize important events in his business that were taking place early on, and he lacked planning.

Planning is extremely important, but, as we have seen over the past few years, even the strongest, largest companies of the '70s and '80s have succumbed to bankruptcy or been reduced to rubble. So for the entrepreneur to fail at his initial venture is certainly nothing to be ashamed of if he gave one hundred percent. However, one business plan is not enough. Having only one plan for a business is like confronting a three-thousand-pound grizzly bear with only one shot in your gun. You had better be extremely accurate!

While planning is important, contingency planning is equally important. Since we recognize now that we cannot control all of the many variables in business all of the time, we can come closer to total control if we employ contingency planning. Contingency planning can address most variables imaginable that pertain to your business endeavor. This is what I refer to as the ability to "bob and weave," kind of like a boxer's mobility to avoid a punch. As a matter of fact, a boxer and a businessman are extremely similar. After all, both are competitive, both must utilize all skills that they have learned, work harder and smarter than their opponents to survive, and be prepared to go the distance.

The contingency could have helped our example in this chapter survive. Not just one, but many contingency plans must be prepared for every turn of events that could effect your business. With this in mind, you will come as close to being in total control of your destiny as possible.

Contingency planning is actually quite easy for the small entrepreneur and often quite difficult for his larger competitors, due to the small guy's ability to bob and weave and respond to the ever-changing business conditions much quicker and more effectively than his larger counterpart. With this in mind, you can see that it is possible for the smaller guy to compete head-to-head with the big guys.

Contingency planning is very important, and you should not attempt your entrepreneurial beginning unless you are prepared to give a lot of thought to the possible variables that could undermine your basic business plan. You will spare yourself a lot of anguish by avoiding the vulnerable areas of new business ventures and by doing your contingency plans. With the contingency plans in place, you will now be able to alter and revise the basic plan at the drop of a hat to accommodate change. Being a one-person enterprise puts you in a far better position than the *Fortune 500* company that has to have a directors' meeting to purchase toilet paper and hold meetings just to schedule more meetings. The big guys might have more capital to work with, but your efficiency level will be absolutely superior.

If by chance you are aiming in some way or fashion at competing with a big guy, it is worth noting that their complacency level has probably set in, and their comfort zones are probably much lower than your own now. Their days of street fighting for market share are over, and that complacent attitude has probably trickled down throughout the organization. They probably do not come close to utilizing their twenty-four-hour day because they get their weekly or monthly pay check, go home, and turn business off. You must work harder and smarter. But the rewards will be incomparable to the amount of compensation your forty-hours-a-week counterparts are realizing.

As mentioned earlier, anyone can lose his or her job, even as the result of mistakes made higher up in management, which is generally the case. Top-level management became complacent enough not to recognize change within their industry to formulate contingency plans that maybe would have adapted to that change without resulting in massive career losses. Well, so much for security!

Don't worry, the price of a job loss was small for the opportunity to become your own person without the reliance on the ineptness of higher management. Please pardon my criticism if you were part of that top layer of management. You can now look forward to unlimited opportunity. The only limits are the preconceived limitations that you place on yourself. Small enterprise is the future, and you are not alone. At this writing IBM has announced the planned reduction of twenty thousand jobs this year, and twenty thousand next year. GM has announced the closing of twentyone factory locations next year. Don't feel like a leper; even the big guys have recognized that small is better.

THINGS TO REMEMBER
1. The basic plan is important, as is the contingency plan.
2. Constantly re-evaluate your plans so that corrective measures can be taken before it is too late.
3. It is far better to expend a little worry and attention to matters early on to avoid a catastrophe later.
4. The ability to "bob and weave" to accommodate change.
5. If you get hit, shake it off early; don't carry it around with you. It may influence your decision-making for the wrong reasons.
6. Treat all issues early on with the survival instinct. We may be human, but it is amazing how much like animals we are when it comes to survival instincts.

APPLYING THE MASTERMIND ALLIANCE

4

The mastermind alliance is a term that I first heard of twenty years ago by reading a publication of *Think and Grow Rich* by Napoleon Hill. This book and others written by Mr. Hill should be bought and studied. His philosophy of business and life is the closest thing that I have read that accurately describes the principles of achieving success. In this chapter we will review the method of applying the mastermind alliance as well as its organization.

The mastermind alliance is just that. It is the alliance of, or formation of, people that are known by you to be experts, or who are at least very knowledgeable on the subjects that will comprise your business operation. They are the specialists in each and every aspect of your endeavor.

In selecting your alliance of people to gain information from, and advise you on your business plans, be selective. Talk with those that you are sure possess the knowledge of the subject matter. These people may not be personal acquaintances of yours.

They may be successful business people who remember their own start-up problems and pitfalls. These are the people you want to seek for advice. Most will be happy, even complimented to talk with you, providing you do not plan to compete with them in their respective fields. A lot of times technical expertise can be obtained from someone currently working for a company already in that particular field.

Now you will become the student by being a good listener and developing the skills of accepting all valued input from those that you choose to surround yourself with. It's important to recognize your role here. You are the orchestra leader, and your mastermind alliance group is your orchestra. You are the central clearing house for information that you receive from your sources. You evaluate the information gathered and make the objective decisions derived from that input. The theory here is that the sum should equal more than the component parts. In other words, you produce the end result, which should be worth far more than each of the components (in this case advice) on its own. The process is much like a computer; you are the computer, and what comes from you is only the result of the input of information that you have received, that valuable information that you have decided to keep and use from your mastermind sources.

One common mistake in pursuing your own destiny is that of calling upon a good friend for his or her advice if that friend is not as progressive and broad-minded as you are. That friend might have a low comfort zone, proud of the fact that he still has a job, but possibly not too anxious to see you break out of the same constraints that have prohibited his major success. Sometimes the common response from a friend when discussing your plans with him will be negative. I have often wondered why this is, and I perceive it as an underlying jealousy of your potential of breaking away from the mediocrity that he is chained to. You can also see by now that your circle of friends may be changing in the future. I for one enjoy limitless thinking people and welcomed my new surrounding with open arms.

An old friend may give numerous examples of why you cannot be successful and mention examples of others who have failed. What makes you think you can do it? Many people have tried, and many people have failed. But for every failure there is the seed of a great reward. You can benefit from those failures by examining them to determine what went wrong. You can benefit by the others' mistakes, and that information is available at no cost. What a deal—a free education at the expense of others. Soak it up like a sponge, but be objective; you will certainly see what their deficiencies were. Now all you have to do is avoid them. You are now far ahead of the pack.

You may not want to disown your friend for his negativeness. His response is a trait that a lot of people possess, and in a couple of years he will probably ask you to join his mastermind alliance group. Offer him a job!

THINGS TO REMEMBER

1. Be selective of whom you let into your mastermind alliance.
2. Total objectivity in evaluating their input is important.
3. Have more than one source of input on each subject and evaluate each argument.
4. Review the total input regularly.
5. Discount bad input and negative response from those whose opinions you do not respect.
6. We all have the ability to associate with only those that we wish to "hang out" with. You want to associate with people who can contribute constructively to your goals. You may be spending less time with old friends.
7. You are the company that you keep!

THE POSITIVE ATTITUDE: GET IT, KEEP IT, USE IT!

5

I've always found the attitudes of the mega-successful businessperson interesting. For the most part, one trait that stands out above all others is his positiveness of direction and purpose. How do you get that positive attitude, especially when confronted with adversity? What I've found from my study on the matter is that it appears to be the same twenty-four hour day. Just as you are the only one who can decide how to spend your twenty-four hours; and just as you are the only one who can decide with whom you choose to associate; that development of the positive attitude principle is the same as our other success traits, inasmuch as you can control it.

To develop the principles, let us look at the thought process. What mechanism is it that lets a thought enter our minds? It is the process of repetitive suggestion. By saying the thought aloud, softly, time after time, repeating it quietly to yourself while lying awake at night, reciting your goals to yourself rather than counting sheep. You must let your goals into your thoughts repetitively through thought, recital, and visualization. Before long, you will learn to master this important process.

In the beginning, after you have identified your goals and objectives, you must, through continued mind visualization, see the end result first. In other words, your business plan may be comprised of four parts, A, B, and C equal money or end result (4). It is important to master the three steps necessary in our example that will produce the fourth part, the end result. What you want to do in the repetitive suggestion procedure is visualize the end result first. This will develop the positive motivational forces necessary for the achievement of the end result. The other component parts can be learned and mastered and will come naturally when called upon to carry out the fulfullment of the end result. But your subconscious must be convinced of your goals by visualizing the end result through repetitive suggestion process. Whatever the mind can conceive and believe, it can achieve; this is an absolute process. Whatever you let enter your thoughts in a repetitive nature, whether true or false, will be believed by the mind in the way that it is presented in repetition. Upon the mind's belief, the end result of achievement will be carried out by your step-by-step plan. You may not even be aware of what is taking shape, but it is.

This principle of positive thought through repetitive suggestion takes some discipline to master. You must think, recite, and imagine your goals and end result taking their tangible form. You must believe your thoughts; therefore, you will be employing two parts of the anatomy: your heart and your mind. If your entrepreneurial field happens to be sales-related, we will touch on the heart-mind relationship in depth in our chapter on career examples. This method of disciplining the subconscious mind to believe through suggestion takes some work to master, but once your goals are conceived it takes only occasional thought to maintain. The process is kind of like training cattle not to leave their pasture by installing an electric wire around it. Every time they touch that wire they get zapped; pretty soon they associate the wire with the zap and will stay put. The subconscious will associate your goals with the components that it knows must be put in place to achieve that goal. You are on auto pilot now!

The subconscious mind can be programmed like a computer to accept as fact what is presented to it. The thoughts that occupy our brain can be controlled. It is only you who allows those thoughts in. The great researcher Napoleon Hill's in-depth study of this principle revealed that one thing that every successful achiever had in common was his ability to let into his thought process only that information which he wanted and to slam the door on negative thoughts. This is not a unique ability, and every person on earth possesses the same power, although many do not use it to its fullest value.

In subconsciously visualizing your success, if

your success definition is making money, you must recite and enter into your thoughts the amount you expect to receive and at what specific time in the future. If you want $100,000 in the bank in two years, visualize that target date and how you perceive your life's change to be at that point in the future. Visualize the lack of economic worry by your loved ones and those around you by visualizing the impact of your success on loved ones, spouses, children, parents, etc. The importance of these loved ones in your life will become your motivating force.

Occasionally, when someone has experienced a failure, he or she tends to dwell on the negative aspect of his or her failure. He or she may reflect on his or her children's faces or spouse's face and become sorrowful and ashamed to have let them down. This type of depressed and negative thinking should and can by wiped from your mind. This depressed state of mind activity takes mental energy, and you can just as easily view an unfortunate event as a fortunate event. Let us examine another attitude toward the same set of circumstances. Your spouse, children, and loved ones are your partners. When times are good you prosper, and they prosper as well. Children are amazing in that they are not as aware of economic status as we are. What they are aware of, though, is the reflection in your face when you become depressed or dwell on failure. A failure should be viewed as a positive experience. Extract from it what you need to analyze mistakes, and learn from it. It is an education that you have paid for;

get some mileage out of it.
 In my situation I was really bummed out initially. What was I going to do? That lasted about one week, and then reality hit home. A light went on in my head. I looked around and saw so many opportunities, especially since I no longer had to answer to anyone. Now I could make some real money. After that first week I recognized that for a long time I had been happy in the machinery business with a small salary plus a one percent commission. Now I had no limit. I knew the people who needed equipment, and I knew the people who had used equipment for sale. I'll never forget my first entrepreneurial deal. A friend of mine had a machine shop in California. This friend called me one day and asked if I knew anyone who needed a silo. I responded that I thought silos were used in Iowa or Nebraska, though I was not sure what they used them for. I had not seen many in California. This man was a casual acqaintance, and I admired him for his horse trader common sense ability. He said, "Jim, I've got this silo on my property that I want to sell. Do you know of anyone that could use it?" Well, silos may be a common sight in Iowa, but let me tell you, they are a rare sight indeed in California. I told him that I had no idea who needed a silo, but he could hop on a plane to the Midwest and probably find a buyer, although the cost of moving it would be enormous. Anyway, I could not waste the time. After all, I had to find a job!
 I'll never forget the only time that I spent in the unemployment office was about twenty min-

utes or less. While I waited in line the day of my initial visit, I began talking to a couple of other guys that appeared, like me, to have something on the ball. After a little conversation about how tough things were, I was the second man in line in front of the window where a fat lady sat interrogating everyone before she gave him or her the check. The guy I had been talking to was at the window. The fat lady grilled this guy as though it were her money, and I could see that her job security was in numbers, the numbers of us who were waiting in line for our handouts. He eventually answered all of her questions and convinced her that he was okay to give some money to. He had his answers down pat because this was his tenth week of collecting that $120. After he had the check from the fat lady in his hot little hands, he turned to walk away, grinned at me, patted me on the shoulder, and said, "See you next week, Jim."

"May I have your forms, sir? May I have your forms, sir?" the deep voice bellowed to me like a drill sergeant. I had momentarily drifted off into the thought of what the guy in front of me had said as he was leaving: "See you next week, Jim." This phrase was bobbing in and out of my mind. Would I see this guy next week? Would we continue our bad luck conversation for the next sixteen weeks or until one of us found a job? Upon the third command from the fat lady in charge of the money, I surrendered my forms. Before she could get the first round of interrogation out of her mouth, I turned and walked away, leaving the lady in charge of my $120 speechless. I knew she

would make it up on the next poor guy.
Driving home, my mind was racing. I should have at least gotten the money, I thought. Although I had a little in the bank, the $120 would have been very helpful, especially since my wife had planned on using it to buy groceries that week.
When I got home, I walked past my wife directly to my office area, where I had a desk and a phone. My wife was ready to go to the grocery store and asked if I had deposited the bread line check into our checking account. As I began dialing the phone, I responded to my wife, asking her to transfer money from savings into checking. She asked why. I told her that I had better things to do than beg for $120 and that the lady and I did not get along very well. My experience at the unemployment line had convinced me that I could spend some time trying to sell my friend's silo, especially after seeing the sales job my friend had to do on the fat lady just to get his money.
The irony of this is that the guy in front of me was so convincing and expended so much energy on the fat lady for his $120 that I was sure that I could devote as much effort to the silo and make more money, maybe a lot more.
I got out the yellow pages of our phone book as I thought of what a silo would be used for. I called Jerry, my friend who wanted to sell the silo, and asked him what they were using it for. He said that the company using it was a plastic bag manufacturer named Crown Zellerbach and that they used it to pump plastic pellets into their

bag-making machines. He said it had two, one-hundred-horsepower dry pumps just like the ones used to pump grain out of grain silos. I told Jerry that I had a buyer, that I wanted two weeks to put the deal together, and that I would give him a $250 deposit to hold it for me for two weeks. He said, "Jim, I want $25,000. Two hundred fifty dollars is only a one percent deposit!" I said, "Jerry, my guy is for real. All I want is your word that it is mine to sell for two weeks!" He then confided that he had given the property owner and new occupants of the Crown Zellerbach building his word that it would be gone in two weeks, and it would take several days to dismantle it. There was no place even to store it. My profit would be any money in the selling price over twentyfive thousand dollars.

When my wife returned home, I asked her to return to the bank and transfer a few hundred more from savings to checking. She responded with, "Why are we hitting our little nest egg so hard?" She also wanted to know where the money from the bread line was. I said, as I frantically thumbed through the yellow pages, that I did not have a lot of time to explain, but the fat lady and I did not get along very well, and I was trying to get the money somewhere else. She sighed, and back to the bank she went. One thing about my wife Karen, she had always given me one hundred percent autonomy in making financial decisions, with no questions asked. As I confronted my new entrepreneurial path uphill, her support, totally without questions as to what I was doing with our nest egg, would be more important than ever.

As I continued to ravage the yellow pages in our local directory for plastic bag manufacturers, I quickly found that there were none. Disappointment began to set in. If I could not find a plastic bag company that would use the silo I had for sale, who was a potential candidate? Then creative thinking took over as if it were on auto pilot. I think that the survival instinct took hold of my thought process, perhaps out of the fear of confronting the fat lady for money again. Now I even called friends in other counties and asked if I could borrow their phone books for a few days. When I drove around to collect all of the phone books that friends agreed to lend me, they always asked why I needed them. I would mumble my plans of putting a silo deal together. I later learned from other friends that after I left they would talk behind my back about how desperate I must be and how glad they were that they still had jobs to go to. This I later learned from other friends. How is this for positive thinking in spite of the negative input from my friends? While this was going on, my wife had total faith in what I was doing. She knew I was a survivor. My daughters, Lori and Cindy, never showed a doubt on their faces. During that silo deal period of time, I had little or no time to talk or communicate with my family, but they saw how driven I was to get this done and knew the situation.

Within a four-county area, I had found one plastic bag manufacturer and about twenty-five plastic molding companies. I called them all about my silo, offering a price of $30,000. (I wanted to net

$5000 for myself.) There were no takers at any price. More discouragement, just what I needed, but I kept the thought process going. Then it clicked. I had been talking to the wrong people. Although bag companies use silos, there was only one bag company in the entire area, and he already had his silo. It was a very limited market indeed.

The next morning at six o'clock I was sitting at my desk. I opened up the first county phone book and turned to the G section. Ga, Ge, Gen, Gr, Gra, and there it was! Grain distributors! What a welcome sight! In Riverside County there were five, in Los Angeles County seven, in Orange County three, and in San Diego County eight. Now I at least had qualified prospects that had bonafide uses for a silo.

The second call I made was to a company by the name of O.H. Kruse Grain & Milling. As I recalled, I had seen their grain trucks quite often on Southern California freeways. I thought that they were probably a big family operation. The operator answered, "O.H. Kruse & Company." "May I speak with Mr. Kruse, please?" I asked in an affirmative voice. The operator responded, "Which Mr. Kruse?" I instinctively replied, "Senior, please!" She came back with, "Who's calling, please?" I replied, "Mr. Waldorf," although I thought that he would surely not recognize the name and would not take the call. I was wrong. The older voice on the other end of the line said, "Oloff Kruse." I realized that I had an audience that I knew used silos and who had lots of them at various locations throughout the state. I liked the fact that I had Mr. Kruse, Sr. on the line and not a son or manager. This was the guy who could make the decisions without committee meetings, and, as I later found out, his humble beginnings were much like my own and we had something in common. This was the man who would shape my destiny and possibly my future, although at the time I did not realize the importance that he represented to me. I addressed him in a congenial manner, sincere and positive, with, "Hello, Mr. Kruse. Thank you for taking my call. Mr. Kruse, I have a silo that must be moved off property in two weeks. It has two, one-hundred-horsepower dry pumps and a 150,000-gallon capacity. Could you use it at one of your locations?" There was a pause between my question and his response of, "How big do you say it is?" "One hundred fifty thousand gallons," I said. "How much do you want?" I gulped as I visualized my $5,000 profit, realizing that it was almost two months' pay and that I had spent a total of three days working on the silo deal. I responded with, "Thirty-two thousand dollars, sir." There was a silence at the other end. My mind was screaming, "That's too much!" What had I done? I became greedy at the last minute and tried to make a $7,000 profit instead of the $5,000 I had fixed in my mind. His silence made me think that I had blown the deal. He came back with, "Where can I send my foreman to see it?" At this point I was ready to do handsprings off the walls. As I held onto my composure, I gave him my phone number and the address of the location of the silo. He said his foreman would meet me at the site the next morning.

I was up at 5:00 a.m., sitting at my calculator figuring out my expenses for the month. House payment $700, car payment $300, groceries $400, utilities $300, gasoline $100, total $1800. That was what I needed to survive the next month. No extras for the kids or for ourselves; this was survival month! The fat lady crossed my mind one more time, as I thought that if I had gotten four $120 payments, I would now have to hit the savings for only $1320 while I invested my time in churning out resumes and went out on interviews that perhaps would land me another "safe, secure" job with a *Fortune 500* company at less money than I had made before. Gee, just think, now instead of socking away $150 per month, I would only be able to save perhaps $100. Isn't that thrilling?

The day of the deal had arrived. My presentation of the silo had to be textbook perfect. The night before, I had read a little about silos, but that morning would be the first time that I would see one up close. I met Mr. Kruse's foreman at 9:00 a.m. He pulled up in a longbed pickup with "O.H. Kruse Company" emblazened on the side. Out stepped a tall, rugged, Midwestern-looking guy. He held out his hand to shake mine, and said, "George Simmons. Are you Jim?" We began tromping down the hill so that he could inspect the silo. I had done some cost comparison on how my $32,000 offer stood up to a brand new 150,000-

gallon silo. New, a replacement would cost $60,000. My price was almost half that; I knew it was fair. While George continued to tromp down the sagebrush hill to inspect the beautiful, shiny, stainless steel silo that beckoned $7,000 to my ears, I made a detour over to Jerry's office to huddle up a game plan with him. He said he would start up the two, one-hundred- horsepower engines so that George could hear them run. Jerry now seemed very anxious, almost nervous, and was obviously in a hurry to get that silo sold and moved out. He now had only ten days to vacate it from the Crown Zellerbach property. The engines began to roar, then backed down to a nice, consistent hum. George crawled under them, over them, and at one point I expected him to pull out a stethoscope to listen to the motor on the left. I thought, "Oh, no, he hears something that isn't right." Maybe I could sacrifice $2,000 of my $7,000 profit to remedy the motor problem that he had found. George waved his hand at Jerry, who was still in the office, to cut the power. Both of the huge motors rumbled to a halt at the same time. George brushed himself off and picked sagebrush splinters out of his white work socks, then walked over to me. He said, "Jim, I'll get back to you this afternoon." I said, "Well, how do they look?" "Well," he said, "they are everything that you said they were to Mr. Kruse. My only question is how soon will we need it." My mind was racing, but I replied quite calmly, "Didn't Mr. Kruse have an immediate need for another silo?" He answered, "Well, not now, but if a good deal comes around we like to take a look, and even if they are not put into service right away, if it's a good enough deal we could save a bundle. I'll call before three," he said, and off into the sunset he rode. In my mind at that point I saw the fat lady beckoning me to her window once again.

As I was returning home, a funny thing happened. I had to drive right past the unemployment office. I noticed a guy that resembled my friend that I stood in line with that terrible day the week before, the guy that said, "See you next week, Jim." This time he was walking away from the unemployment office and into the cocktail lounge next door. It was only 11:00 a.m., and I couldn't help but think, why is a guy out of work drinking at eleven o'clock in the morning? He seemed to be a halfway knowledgeable person and a good enough salesman to convince the fat lady to give him his $120. As a matter of fact, I perceived him to be an excellent salesman. I thought that he probably could have sold that silo better than I was attempting to do. So why was this guy content with making one sales presentation a month for $120? If my silo deal happened, I would make $7,000 in four days. See the risk-reward ratio? When I saw this guy walking into the cocktail lounge, I thought that if I had stopped by the bread line this morning I would be walking in with my new-found associate, and perhaps the bartender would have a ckeck cashing service and for a threepercent fee he would cash our unemployment checks. With this thought in mind, I believe that I would hold a higher degree of professional respect for the bartender. At least he might have been enterprising enough to turn a profit, recognizing how important it is to produce income. With all of these thoughts going through my mind, I could now see how fragile a person's direction in life could be. Mr. Kruse's decision that afternoon would obviously determine whether I could choose the path of least resistance or the path that was slightly more difficult but possessed a far greater reward. If anything, exercise in entrepreneurship would be a good workout.

At 3:20 my phone rang. I answered on the first ring. It was, as I expected, George from O.H. Kruse. He said, "Mr. Waldorf, we will pay $16,000 for your silo, and our crew will have it dismantled and moved off the property within seven days, well before your deadline." I responded, "Well, George, I had expected to get a little closer to a fair price." He responded by saying that he really did not need a silo right away and that they would be putting it into storage until a need arose, which might be several years. He also pointed out that with the heavy cranes that would need to be involved in the dismantling process, it would be difficult to meet the deadline without devoting a very large crew to the project, but he was prepared to do that if I accepted the offer. I asked if I could call him right back, and he obliged. As soon as I hung up, the phone rang again. This time it was Jerry, whom I had planned on calling. He said, "Jim, did your guys buy the silo?" I began to tell him of their offer, but I bit my tongue and said that no, I had not heard from them yet, but I would give them a call and get back to him. He said that was okay, but that it was really important that he get that silo out of there. When I hung up from Jerry I evaluated the deal for a while. Number one, Jerry seemed awfully anxious when he called. Did I know how much money Jerry had in the silo? No, I did not. Within twenty minutes I called Jerry back. I said, "Jerry, I can only get you $8,000 for the silo." At this point I held the receiver about twelve inches away from my ear to avoid being deafened by his response. "What the h—-! That thing is $60,000 new!" I said, "Jerry, it is going to take a big crew a lot of hours to get that thing dismantled and moved. Do you want the deal?" He responded with, "Can you get me a cashier's check in the morning?" I said yes. He said, "Okay, it is yours." I was numb when I got off the phone. I had sold the silo for less than half of the original price quoted to the customer and had made $8,000 instead of the $5,000 or $7,000 at the higher level. Now all I had to do was get $8,000 to pay Jerry tomorrow. I only had about $4,500 in savings. I called George back and said, "George, I will take your offer; however, here are the conditions: I will deliver a bill of sale to your office in the morning and pick up a check for fifty percent of the purchase price at the same time, with the balance due when you begin the dismantling." He said, "Come on over."

The next morning I prepared a bill of sale with the serial numbers that Jerry had given me off the silo, picked up an O.H. Cruse check, deposited it at their bank, and had an $8,000 cashier's check drawn to Jerry. I carried the check out to Jerry personally and asked him to confirm the serial number on the bill of sale. He said, "Let's walk on down to the silo and see." When we got to the silo, he pulled out a hammer and a set of number stamps and proceeded to look at the number on the bill of sale and to stamp those same numbers on the silo. He shook my hand and said, "Jim, you sure got me off the hook on this deal." I was a little confused about his statement, and if anything I had expected him to be a little disgruntled; after all, he had gotten only one-third of the price that he originally asked for the silo. Then he confided in me that Crown Zellerbach were the owners of the silo and the property and that he had been contracted by them and paid $10,000 to dismantle and get rid of the silo before the new owner of the bag building took possession. They had already paid him $10,000 to throw it away! I was glad to hear the essence of the entire deal, because every single person involved benefited. Jerry made $18,000 for doing nothing, I made $8,000 for doing everything, O.H. Kruse saved $44,000 over the price of a new silo, and Crown Zellerbach got the monster out of their hair on time. Whew, what a deal! On day number five, I had earned $8,000, and I did earn it, almost three months' pay from my big secure job as Western Regional Sales Manager, and only one week since I declined the handout at the unemployment office.

THINGS TO REMEMBER
1. Read the example deal a few times, and note the mechanics.
2. Master the visualization of where you want to be in the future.
3. Avoid association with negative people.
4. Seek only the company of positive, progressive people.
5. You control what enters your thoughts; only allow positives.
6. When that negative does appear through the cracks, turn it around so that only positives that exists in it are seen. An example of this is the following: UNEMPLOYMENT—is a negative thing happening to you? It is a great opportunity! You no longer must answer to anyone. Now you have time to make real money, as well as steer your own ship for a while.

In this chapter I hit pretty hard on not accepting unemployment benefits. I refused to accept them; however, this does not mean that you should do the same. Your economic situation will dictate whether you should cut the tie or not.

If you are accepting benefits or are underemployed, I would hope that you are not a patron of the Tony's Tavern hard-luck story group. This is a nonproductive way of passing your hours. It is not just the time spent in the bar that you are losing; it is the time that you have left as well because you have an impairment to deal with for the next several hours, and at this time in your life you must be as sharp and accurately thinking as you possibly can be.

A NOTE TO YOUR SPOUSE:
Pay attention to the loyalty and faith philosophy outlined in this chapter. Your mate is attempting a journey that will pay off economically as well as emotionally. Stand behind him or her. He or she needs you now more than ever before. There is an eternal law on this subject: Be prepared to give all to accomplish your goals, and your goals will be realized.

7. Keep in mind that although in my personal example I made $8,000 in only five days, this cannot be thought of as a cushion. If you think that it is, your comfort zone is way too low, and you might as well throw this book away or return it for a refund because you do not have what it takes in the discipline department to master your own destiny.

Now is not the time to buy that new television just because you have three months' income on hand. Take your profit from every deal and bank it for at least the first year and perhaps for two years. Only spend to service your existing obligations. You may need the money; remember, you no longer have that set amount each week or each month, and now you must insulate yourself from economic failure of any kind. Above all, don't stop now just because you have earned a few dollars. You've only just begun.

ISN'T IT GREAT BEING HERE AT THE BOTTOM

6

As absurd as this statement must sound to most, when you really take a very close look at the advantages of being at the bottom, the true light begins to shine through. Everything in business is measured by risk versus reward, just like the casinos in Las Vegas. The only difference is that you don't have the lights and dancing girls.

To give an example of what I mean by how great it is to be at the bottom, keep in mind that when you are in that position on the ladder in business entrepreneurship or life in general, your upside potential is far greater than that of the guy at the top. You have a greater chance to advance upward on the ladder than the guy at the top does. Let us evaluate that guy at the top. What are his chances for downside risk? Very good indeed. As you progress up the ladder, notice that the steps become narrower and harder to maintain a footing on. But at the bottom of a step ladder, the steps are nice and wide and easy to climb until you reach the top of the pyramid, and then you are in a very vulnerable spot indeed.

If your planned entrepreneurship takes you on the path of competing with your former employer (and this seems to be a popular path for a lot of people because they are already familiar with that enterprise), keep this example in mind. Just like the old cliche, "the bigger they are, the harder they fall." This had never been so true as in our example of the business and entrepreneurial ladder.

It is very easy to double your income each year for the first few years, but that compound growth rate does not go on forever. Eventually it does slow down, level off, and then decline. The amount of the decline or the length of time in the levelling-off period entirely depends upon your bob and weave ability. As mentioned in the previous chapter, mobility and the ability to change soon enough to accommodate changing conditions in your business will determine the length and breadth of your climb as well as your descent in business.

Changes affecting your business or profession must be recognized early on so that your contingency planning can be put into play. Don't limit yourself, however, to your prepared or conceived contingency plans alone. There may very well be variations to those plans that would be more adequate to your change. In other words, always be open to other methods as well as change. Don't succumb to tunnel vision; look all around you at every opportunity available, then let your evaluation skills weigh the risk-reward ratio, and call upon your mastermind alliance for their input.

Three years ago a friend of mine mentioned that he had just received notice that the company that he had worked for for twenty-four years was putting him out to pasture—not retirement, but getting rid of him. He had been their western regional salesman. The company was a supplier of chocolate to companies that used bulk chocolate. This seems like a pretty big market to me: ice cream manufacturers, candy makers, bakeries, etc. Don was bummed out pretty badly over the loss of his $60,000-per-year job. At this particular time, I had been doing my own thing for eight years, and Don knew that I had been fairly successful as an independent entrepreneur coming from the same bad break experience that he was now confronted with. He came to me for advice one day, and we attempted to develop a plan for Don to "land on his feet" at this particular time in his life. Don was fifty-three years old but still had many good earning years to devote his talent to, and he was not financially prepared to retire for good.

Don had asked me to become a part of his mastermind alliance by going over a lot of things that he had questioned regarding my own business success. Don was given information, all of which is contained in the book you are now reading. My advice to him was exactly what I am outlining for you, but you have the benefit of having it in print to refer to readily when necessary.

In counseling Don I pointed out what a great thing it was not to be hassled by the national sales manager anymore, not to have to take a full day out of every week just to prepare a stupid written sales report outlining whom you visited, what you talked about, and then predicting (like a clairvoyant) when the guy would buy, as well as how much. What a great blessing not to have to conform to unproductive, non-revenue-producing, time wasting methods of big enterprise. Now as an entrepreneur, the order will get there when it gets there, no sooner, no later, as simple as that, end of story.

During our conversation I could see Don start to relate with entrepreneurial methods and thinking. He was an intent listener who had the maturity to master everything that was outlined for him. I had absolutely no doubt that this man had been severely underemployed in the income department for twenty of the twenty-four years he had worked for his company. He had every single characteristic that was necessary for success. After several meetings he decided to begin his plan as an independent sales representative within his former industry. He did, as I recall, collect some unemployment checks for a short time until his first commission check arrived.

I enjoyed seeing the path that Don took. He went directly to his former employer's competitor, which was located on the east coast and had very little market presence in the western U.S. He asked them for the right to sell as an independent in seven western states on a commission-only basis of ten percent. Within six months Don's income from commissioned sales of the one product line totalled $45,000. He was on his way to a $90,000 year, fifty percent more than his best year with his secure job. How would you like to be able to give yourself a fifty-percent raise in one year?

Since Don's beginning three years ago, he has confided that he has branched out into other food-related lines as well and that his income for last year was $140,000. Not too bad for a guy who was feeling down and out as recently as thirty-six months ago. Another thing worthy of mentioning that I truly enjoy hearing about is that he has had numerous phone calls from his former employer requesting a meeting. Needless to say, he has had no interest whatsoever!

In evaluating Don's cirumstances you might ask why he was let go from his former employer. It appeared that they felt that they had such a strong market presence in the West that they would maintain their orders by phone and no longer needed the guy that devoted twenty-four years of his life in putting them on the map. As you know, this is not uncommon at all. Don was able not only to land on his feet, but I would say that after our meetings early on, he landed on the track running!

Now Don is working his way up the ladder, and his former employer is on its way down the other side. I could not think of a more graphic example of how great it is to be at the bottom than Don's.

Another example of working up from the bottom is the career of my friend Steve. I met Steve about fifteen years ago. He was involved in a very unglamorous business: he collected waste paper from trash bins, dump sites, and other places that he could find old paper. Steve's father was a buyer for a large paper company that manufactured new paper as well as recycled paper. Steve sold his waste paper in loose form, not compressed or baled, to local paper mills. It took many trips to make a little money. You see, waste paper is bought by the ton, so it is very important to have the heaviest load possible on your truck to amortize the costs of shipping. Steve and I grew up in the same city although our paths had not crossed until we were in our late twenties. I watched Steve work hard and smart as he climbed the ladder of success. I remember when he got his first paper baling machine. With his new machine he could compress the paper that he had previously hauled loose into tight, dense, heavy bales. This enabled him to load big truck and trailer rigs to the maximum, weight-wise, for shipping to the paper mills. Then he bought property that he once rented and gradually convinced the major paper mills to give him a try. Eventually the biggest mills in the country began calling Steve for tonnage to feed their huge operations and giving him long-range orders for tonnage in the future as well. If Steve did not have the tonnage, he would find it among his competitors and purchase it from them to be shipped directly to the mills. Eventually Steve had the long-term commitments from the mills that his much larger competitors previously had, and they found themselves selling their production to Steve.

Steve was gradually climbing the ladder from ground zero as his much larger competitors were not only losing market share but calling Steve to buy their waste paper, to resell to the customers that they once sold to before Steve came on the scene. In a few short years he had three yard locations in Southern California. Peddlers in pickup trucks as well as large metro newspaper publishers like the L.A. *Times* were selling their excess paper to his locations, where it was baled into heavier weights and trucked to mills all over the country. Today Steve has several yard locations throughout the western United States. As his competitors' businesses fell off, he bought their yard locations, often keeping top level management intact and occasionally offering employment to the former owners. Today he has offices all over the world that trade his waste paper to paper mills. He now not only loads paper onto trucks for the trips to domestic mills, but he also loads it onto ships to be transported to mills throughout the world. I would estimate Steve's revenue to be in the area of $160,000,000 this year, and I imagine it will be twice that by the end of the nineties.

I consider Steve my best friend, although our businesses are so unrelated that we see each other only a few times per year. Several years back I recruited him as part of my mastermind alliance. During that period we played tennis five nights a week and attended lots of social events that were geared for his industry. He also allowed me into high-level negotiations and business meetings within his business, knowing that I had a thirst to learn more about success for myself.

One of my early entrepreneurial dealings was the commission sales of equipment that was used at the scrap metal division of Bethlehem Steel Company's Los Angeles steel-making division. When they closed in the early eighties, I approached them about trusting me to find markets for their used equipment. They agreed to pay a ten-percent commission on equipment that I sold for them. My contacts in this industry were the steel scrap processing companies throughout the country that I had befriended during my employment with the big, secure company I had been laid off from and which is no longer in business after an over one hundred year existence. I had sold off most of the equipment that was to be disposed of in about six months, all but one machine that I simply could not find a buyer for. They approached me on an outright purchase; in other words, they wanted me to buy it for resale. I was complimented but I did not have sufficient cash to give them. I called Steve and asked if he wanted to go in as a partner in the deal. He asked how much it would be. I went back to Bethlehem, and they said that they wanted what they showed it on their books to be worth (depreciated value). Well, if you know something about depreciation, you can see that a five-year-old machine may be stated very low on their balance sheet. I was right; they showed its depreciated value as only $18,000. I had thought that they would want at least $75,000.

I told Steve that I would put up $9,000 if he would do the same, and we would split the profit fifty-fifty when I found a buyer. He agreed right away, as I knew he would, but gave me instructions to research the replacement cost if somebody had to buy the same machine new. I called the manufacturer, the Constellation Shear Co. They said that a new model XYZ machine was $580,000! This machine was five years old, and I could buy it for $18,000. Surely I would be able to fetch $100,000 for it within a reasonable time frame.

I told Steve what I had learned about its replacement cost. He told me to go over to his bank the next morning and that they would have a $25,000 cashier's check ready for me. I said that it was only $9,000 for his half and that he must have been thinking of another deal with a $25,000 figure. I'll never forget his response. He said, "Jimmy, I am in a better position than you to risk money. You are doing the work. You brought the opportunity to me. Don't short-change yourself. You offered a partnership in the transaction, but no deal can be lopsided and disproportionate where one person benefits more than another. I am the money guy, and you are doing the work; that is a fair partnership." I said, "Well, why $25,000? They want $18,000." He said that he knew the numbers but that I was going to need incidental money for moving, cleaning, and storage. The following day I bought our investment for $18,000, then hired dismantlers to take it apart and four trucks to haul it to a location that I had rented.

During this period of time I was also publishing an equipment newsletter that was mailed to scrap-metal processors throughout the country. In a short period of time, I had gotten over three hundred pieces of equipment listed in my newspaper. What made my publication unique was that I did not charge to advertise. That's right. What I did was charge between a six-percent and ten-percent commission on the sale of a piece of equipment. There was no risk to the seller as far as the cost of his ad; only on performance of a sale at his price did I collect a commission, which was far more than I would have made charging for ads. I had control of the seller as well as the buyer because anything I listed in my paper could only be seen by calling my toll-free phone number, not the seller's number. Thus, no one ever went around me. When I had the five-year-old Constellation scrap shear for sale, I devoted a full page to advertising it in my *Green Sheet Equipment Journal* at a price of $100,000. Within two weeks I had a call from a gentleman in Minnesota whom I later found out was not only a very large scrap processor in that area but a large shareholder in American Motors. He asked if my $100,000 was firm. I answered no. He said he would be out later in the week to see it. Three days later I picked him up at the airport and drove him out to see the machine. He said, "I'll pay $75,000 and no more." I said, "You have a deal!" Within seven days I wrote Steve a check for $50,000. I had doubled his investment and earned $25,000 for myself. The reason I am telling this story is that it touches on an important dimension in achieving success. That is, there is no such thing as a successful transaction unless all people involved benefit. This is especially true if you want longevity in an industry or profession. Steve pointed out that I should not be using my own money; I should be using his. My fifty percent was earned from finding and making the deal happen and his from putting capital at risk. He wanted it that way so that later on I would not look back and think that I had done all the work when we had each put up half the money. Steve had clearly taught me a very important success principle in fairness and long-term thinking that I have always remembered and practiced myself. To this day I know that if I ever need a very deep pocket to carry out a business deal, I need only to pick up the phone, although I do not anticipate such a need. I was very fortunate in having the opportunity of surrounding myself with Steven's business expertise and to have learned from him.

THINGS TO REMEMBER

1. Being at the bottom is great! This positive attitude is the ONLY way you can view being at the bottom. Look at how much upside potential you have to look forward to.

2. As your own entrepreneurial success excels, remember that the larger you become, the sooner it is that you will become vulnerable to a plateau and then a decline.

3. You can control the duration of the plateau or downside, but you must continually monitor and review as well as listen to feedback from all

sources, especially customers. At the earliest sign of my good friend Steve's imposing a threat to the paper industry being controlled, his big competitors should have made him an offer. As it stands, most of them now work for him on property that they once owned.

4. A one-time deal without looking back and without concern for all people involved is a short-sighted mentality, and it will catch up with you eventually. A lot has been written on this "win, win" theory of all parties' benefiting from a transaction. Do not make enemies, and do not burn bridges!

LANDING ON YOUR FEET 65

WHY DO YOU WANT ALL THAT MONEY?

7

If this question were put to most people, the answer would most likely range the following reasons: to ensure security for oneself and family, to get a new car, to buy a new house, to help pay for an education, etc. Well, all of these are very good reasons to desire money. One answer that will probably never come up is simply to have the tangible money stacked in piles to fill a room to the ceiling. It is reasonably accurate, then, to say that virtually nobody wants money just to have the money.

Money is only a medium of exchange, a method of trading in a common denomination to acquire all of the things listed above. Money can only be wanted for its purpose, and one really does not want money but the things that money can buy.

Let us take this argument a step further now and ask ourselves why we want the things that money can buy. There is a universal answer to this question, but few would have the answer. We want the things that money can buy because it makes us feel good. Now you may say that is not true, that you want some money for your son's operation or for your daughter, to make them feel good and that it is not for you. By providing this for them, it also makes you feel very good, though, doesn't it?

There is nothing wrong with the reason that we desire to accumulate the money that can get us the things that make us feel good. It is not selfish to want to feel good; it is basic human nature.

Money is intended to be used for the benefit of people. It is important to save but not to hoard. You will recognize that, by putting money into circulation, especially as a business investment, you will help many people by providing employment and opportunities for them to learn. By spending money at the local mall, you are keeping a retail clerk at his or her job as well as keeping the manufacturer producing the goods that you are buying.

In the earlier chapter on visualizing the rewards that you expect to receive from your new enterprise, most of us would not visualize rooms full of twenty- and fifty-dollar bills stacked to the ceiling. What most would envision would be the tangible effects of the accumulation of money, new cars, new homes, peace of mind, etc. Yes, peace of mind is a tangible just like the car and house. After all, it makes us feel good as well, and probably makes us feel better than all of the toys and other tangibles put together. A lot of times, peace of mind, as you well know, cannot be purchased.

As you have surmised, money is a very strange and often elusive commodity. Our reasons for wanting it sometimes are also viewed as strange if you were to compare our living conditions in the U.S. to those of other countries such as Guatemala, where the father of a little girl we sponsor through Children International makes twelve dollars per month and supports a family of five.

A lot of times someone's motivation for money will be for the examples of tangible items that I have mentioned, and there are many that were not mentioned. Let us look a little closer and examine why these things are so important to some people that priorities seem to be screwed up.

Take the guy who buys a new sports car and encumbers himself with a debt load that costs him $700 or $800 per month while he has a hard time paying his phone bill or rent. Why does he place a higher priority on this car? Well, he may claim that he loves the way it handles, he may claim that he is a real car buff and truly appreciates a car of this nature, although it is highly unlikely that his car could be viewed as an investment that is expected to increase in value, in fact he is probably losing money in depreciation by the hour. Why does this guy have such a misalignment of priorities? Well, we all have a self-image that we believe best portrays who we are to others. The sports car this fellow bought was a reflection of that self-image. Sometimes a person's self-image, the image that he has of himself, is entirely different than the way that he actually is. The guy with the new sports car is portraying on the surface a megabuck image, although in fact he is not close to the image that he expects people to believe. Kind of a charade, isn't it? Human nature suggests that a lot of us want to be viewed or perceived in a certain way, even though that way is not at all the way that we really are.

On the other hand, there are plenty of times when people may perceive us as being entirely different than the way we actually are. An experience that comes to mind first is one that I encountered as a teenage boy. I believe I was thirteen or fourteen years old at the time. I had gone over to visit another kid in our neighborhood who lived a few blocks away. As I walked to the door, I heard his mother talking to another neighborhood kid's mother about various kids in the neighborhood. As I recall they were generally pretty critical of them. When she got to me, she said, "And that Jim Waldorf! What a troublemaker he appears to be. I don't know if I like having my Bernie hang around with him." I had just started to lift my hand to knock on the door when I heard this statement. Instead of knocking I turned and walked back home. I recall being far more sensitive as a kid than I am as an adult, and that statement at the time really hurt me. I've always wondered what image I had portrayed to prompt this lady to judge me. I am at a total loss to answer that. It is worth noting, though, that little Bernie and I seemed to associate less and less after that, and we eventually lost contact altogether as we entered our upper teenage years. I heard, however, that about the same time that I began my first business venture at age twenty-three, Bernie was serving a fifteen-year debt in the California prison system for armed robbery along with another kid from the old neighborhood. This is just one example of being perceived and judged incorrectly by someone.

We are all subject to being judged by another's perception of us, which could be very different from the way that we really are. This is why it is important to consciously put forth the image that you think best describes yourself to the world. This is particularly true in a sales professional's environment. You should dress, groom, and carry yourself the way that you want to be viewed in business. People more often than not do judge the book by its cover.

Another example on the same matter was given by Napoleon Hill in one of his studies. Mr. Hill was visiting a plantation owner in the South, and they were in the barn one day. The plantation owner stood six feet, five inches tall and weighed in at about 235 pounds, had a huge, dark, full beard and in general appeared to be quite scary. As Hill and the owner talked, the owner began to go to work sharpening a huge ax on the foot-pedalled sharpening stone. As sparks began to fly in the dark, damp barn, a light peered through a small crack in the doorway which had been closed when they walked in. The owner looked up and there stood in silence a little black girl perhaps six or seven years old who was wearing a tattered and torn dress. She stared at the big plantation owner until he acknowledged her with, ''What do you

you want in here?" in a deep, snarly voice that would have scared the crap out of most grown men. The little girl took one step forward and replied, "My mama wants fifty cents." Apparently the little girl's mother worked for the plantation owner. The big guy said, "You'll get nothing from me today. Now get out of here," and he raised his huge arm up and pointed at the door. Right after that statement he looked back down at his sharpening stone and began to go about his business of finishing the grind on his ax. A minute or so later, he finished his project, glanced up, and, to his astonishment, the little black girl had budged not an inch after his ordering her out of the barn. Now the big guy appeared outraged as he stormed toward the little girl, waving his arms and shouting, "Out of here, I said!" When he got within two feet of the little girl, she stood her ground, leaned her little body forward, chin out in front, with her arms straight behind her at her sides and said, "But I told you my mama's got to have that fifty cents." To Hill's surprise, that little forty-five pound girl stood up to someone that most would perceive as a very scary and mean person. The big guy dug deeply into his right pocket and came out with a fifty-cent piece and gently handed it to the little girl, and within a split second she was out of there.

The example shows the little girl's willingness to accept possible injury from that big scary plantation owner to receive what her mother had sent her for. The little girl knew that she absolutely had to have that fifty cents and was not going anywhere (on her own) until she got it. Here she saw through an image of a tough guy and reduced him to rubble. The tough plantation owner perceived and judged the little black girl entirely wrong, but possibly by the cover.

THINGS TO REMEMBER

1. Nobody wants money for what it is, but only for what it can offer.

2. As you begin to accumulate good income, remember that you may be called upon to put some back in to keep your enterprise running well.

3. There is no such thing as stealing from yourself. As your income begins to rise, think twice before buying that sports car. Be frugal until you are really financially invincible. I don't know anyone who would knock a person who drives a ten-year-old car but who has a fat bank account. But the guy who has the $800 per month debt on his sports car and cannot pay his phone bill had better sit himself down and get to know himself a little better.

4. Remember how important it is to be perceived by those you intend to do business with in the way that you want them to view you. If it appears that you are making too much money, some people may reject you because of that. I know that I always let my customers feel slightly superior to me. They do not know that I am doing this, but if you feed a guy's ego, you've made him feel good, and whom do people want to do business with? You got it: those of us who make them feel good. Be very careful about how you

portray your economic status in business. It is a double-edged sword. There are many times I leave my Mercedes in the garage and drive my Jeep or my Ford.

5. Visualize the actual reasons that you want to make a lot of money. Ingrain that vision on your subconscious mind through the repetitive process. Visualize the tangible rewards for your hard work as well as your step-by-step plan to accumulate it.

ENTREPRENEURIAL EXAMPLES TO RELATE TO

8

In this chapter I would like to tell of first-hand entrepreneurial examples of people that I personally know who have succeeded in the face of apparent failure. What I find extremely interesting to note is that of all the examples I have outlined, and of all the many others I personally know who were down and out and came back to achieve success in view of previous failures, every single one has done extraordinarily well; and there is absolutely no comparison to the income levels they made when they were working for someone else.

Although my friend Steve Young, who controls a healthy portion of the recycled paper fibers in the U.S. waste paper industry, has already been mentioned, there are quite a number who have been as successful in many other fields. One who comes to mind is a lady by the name of Sally Stanford, who unfortunately passed away of natural causes in 1987 or so at the ripe old age of seventy-nine.

I met Sally for the first time in 1980, while I

was waiting for friends to join me for dinner at the Valhalla Restaurant in Sausalito, California. She was sitting at the bar in this upscale restaurant at the other end of the Golden Gate Bridge that connects to San Francisco. Sally was sitting in a barber's chair at the very end of the bar, and the chair was obviously reserved for her. She looked at me after I had sat there about thirty minutes nursing a scotch, after having been called to my table twice. She asked if I were waiting for someone to arrive from San Francisco. I said that I was waiting and that I was a little concerned about them now that they were thirty minutes late. She told me that she had just heard that the Golden Gate Bridge was closed due to an accident and a total fog-in and that they would most likely be quite late. About that time I was paged at the bar. My friend was calling from his car phone right in the middle of the traffic accident, where a policeman estimated it would be 9:30 before he could get across to Sausalito. My friend suggested that we have dinner tommorrow night instead. I agreed. The lady in the barber's chair had heard my conversation on the bar phone and at that time summoned a waiter and whispered in his ear some instructions as she glanced my way. The waiter nodded dutifully and walked off to set up a table with the very best panoramic view of San Francisco. As she walked over to my seat at the bar, I wondered who this very congenial old gal, dressed in a full sequined gown with red leather pumps and a little more makeup than most gals wear, was. She asked if I would like to join her table for dinner since my friends had stood me up. I thought for sure that this lady was someone who had something interesting to say because of the respect that she had around that restaurant, and I was eager to be her student for dinner.

We talked for two hours about philosophy. She told me about her cat named Tom that was going to Chicago to have kidney surgery at a cost of $25,000. She asked what I was doing in the area. I told her of the machinery that I sold to scrap metal processors throughout the country and how interesting I had found the scrap metal guys to be. In their quest for survival as Jewish immigrants, they had developed huge empires worth fortunes today. She told me of her son who was a prominent attorney and of his wife, whom she believed was after her estate when she was gone. She had considered leaving her entire estate to her cat, Tom, including the famous Valhalla Restaurant which she had owned for many, many years. She began to tell me of a film she was involved in, as an advisor to the producers of a movie for television that was the autobiography of her life. In the film, a movie called *The Lady of the House*, Dyan Cannon played the role of Sally Stanford. Sally became the most successful proprietor of a brothel ever. She catered to upscale, famous people, all of whom are talked of in her written autobiography of *The Lady of the House*.

Sally was a poor girl from southern Oregon who migrated south to the San Francisco area during the heyday of oil exploration and the gold rush days. Here brothels catered to movie stars of that era as well as to politicians. This is an entrepreneurial example that I would not recommend to anyone reading this book, but it does say something about the poor girl from Oregon whom I visited at least three different times a year until her death. Every time I saw her she was wearing a different pair of red high heels; as she pointed out in her autobiography, the first thing she remembered ever wanting really badly as a girl was a pair of red, high-heel shoes. She obviously achieved her visualized goal as well as much more. Her wealth was held in a lot of property throughout the bay area and other parts of the country and of course the old Valhalla Restaurant, where she befriended strangers who were stood up and made them a part of her life and a part of history as well.

Sally endured hard times and survived. I have no opinion of the way that she accomplished her goals of accumulating seed money to begin her other legitimate enterprises. For her accomplishments I respect her, and though my gut reaction is not willing to accept her early methods, they did work for her. Her past did come back to haunt her later in life as it ruined her marriage to a very prominent Bay Area attorney, a man she loved very much, whose sister was bent on exposing Sally after she had gotten out of the business. The sister uncovered scandalous facts that eventually ruined her marriage.

What Sally's advice to me on life was, "Jim, if you are ever being run out of town, just get in front of the crowd that's at cause, and make like you're leading a parade." I still think about Sally's advice from time to time, and what I have concluded about the life and times of my friend Sally Stanford is that standing in line at the fat lady's window in the 1930s must have been far worse than it is today.

Another example more realistic in nature and more practical than Sally's experience at entrepreneuring it is my friend Dan Diorio, with whom I am also associated in our nine-year-old machinery sales business.

Dan was a service technician who worked for an electronic control manufacturer out of New Jersey. He would fly out to the West Coast to work on the machinery that had been equipped with Slo Syn controls. These controls were installed on machine shop equipment to program from a blue print the configuration of a part that would now drive the motion that the machine must go through to manufacture the part. This was ground-floor automation of the industrial sector of the U.S. during the mid- to late 70s.

Dan was never just a service guy. He was an astute student of what this book is all about. Dan Diorio is truly, unquestionably, a limitless person. The word "can't" does not exist in his vocabulary. After a few years of working on the machines that his company's salesmen sold, he noticed that the salesmen generally drove nicer cars, had more money to spend, dressed better, and had more fun, while Dan was the guy that made them look like heroes by keeping the equipment humming along, which meant the success or failure of the next sale. Dan saw an opportunity that was ground-floor in nature and which had a lot of upside potential for someone who was not afraid of hard work and who had the tenacity of handling rejection well. That was Dan. His philosophy today is still the same as mine: there are twenty-four hours in a day—why succumb to mediocrity by doing like other salesmen and eating lunch from eleven o'clock to two in the afternoon, staying home one day a week to do sales reports that their bosses want to see? In other words, we do not subscribe to the forty-hours-per-week mentality. Your productive hours are only about twenty hours per week. We all have the same amount of time; the only difference is that we work hard during our time. The end of the month is going to be here regardless of whether you worked super-human hard or took it easy. The only difference is that with us, we have more money than ninety percent of the other salesmen in our industry. As you can see, the work ethic is a real key. Dan decided to accept a job offer from a very large machine tool distributor called the Hasbach Company. He took a chance and moved his family out West to pursue a career in sales.

Dan was raised on the East Coast, so this was a pretty big move for him and his wife, Jackie, who was a Toronto lady herself. Growing up for Dan was tough because of his father's untimely death when Dan was very young. Now all were coming West to seek their fortune.

Going to work for the Hasbach company, Dan

was given a base salary plus a percentage. He had a very large territory with a lot of machine shops. Early out Dan asked the company to eliminate his security blanket, the base that ninety percent of salesmen want to have, but to increase his commisssion percentage; in other words, to pay him more on performance. They agreed.

With the discipline of cold-calling on twenty shops per day, Dan developed what he calls the five-minute sales call. He walks into the machine shop, seeks out the owner, gets in front of him, and asks the important questions, such as, "When are you going to update your old equipment with my new modern equipment?" He would get the response, and if it appeared he had the guy thinking, he would devote some more time. If the guy said he would replace in about six months, Dan would see him at least once a month from then on. Then down the road he would go to the next five-minute sales call. He recognized and worked the numbers theory.

Dan's ability to work hard and to read between the lines in looking for signals from the customer is supernatural. We have both indentified that most of the time what the potential customer tells you is not all the truth. It is up to you to read between the lines. With this success principle, Dan Diorio and I have sold more machinery than any other two people in the world. Our combined career totals are in excess of seven thousand machines sold, at an average price of $60,000, for a total of about $420,000,000 in sales. We earned from three to six percent in commissions on each sale. Occasionally, early on, we got eleven percent, for about $6600 in commission per $60,000 machine. Dan and I had many fifteen-machine months. Commissions of $40,000 per month became quite common for me; Dan consistently outproduced me and has had many million-dollar years.

A company that Dan and I appoached to sell their machines back in 1982, Fadal Engineering Company, agreed to let us sell their newly developed machining centers throughout Southern California on a commission-only basis, as we like it. Fadal has been featured in recent business publications of *Business Week* as a company that was able to capture eighty percent of the domestically built machining center market and to reverse a two-decade-old trend of Japanses control of that market. That is quite an accomplishment for a small, privately owned company. I am really proud to have had the opportunity of associating with the Decaussin brothers, the three sons of Francis Decaussin, a Detroit machinist who moved to California and became an entrepreneur by opening his own machine shop in 1957 with his son Larry after both of their paychecks from their employer bounced. Their rationale was that if they were going to take a chance on the check's being good, they might as well take a chance in their own business and steer their own ship. The Decaussins truly landed on their feet in taking control of the U.S. machining center market with sales of $130,000,000 in 1991, up from $3,000,000 in 1984. How's that for growth? Now they must be concerned about plateau and decline as they face the challenge of what to do for an encore.

Here is how Dan Diorio and I view commission-only sales situations: it is great! If your planned entrepreneurial path is in sales, you can throw away that security blanket called a base and rely on your ability by negotiating a fair sales commission and a lucrative enough potential territory. I can say, and many of my machine tool sales associates can also say, that we will never be working for someone else again. The sales manager today has no value.

Remember that if you are working for a sales manager that he may offer you two options. Plan number one might give you $2,000 per month with a two-percent commission, while plan number two would give you no monthly base with a five-percent commission. Take the second plan, which will clearly establish you as an independent contractor. You will soon realize your full potential.

Dan Diorio is clearly the number-one machine tool salesman in the world, both in income and number of machines sold. I have the dubious distinction of being number two in the world in income but number one in the world in the last five-year period in number of machines sold. I will tell you my personal story of entrepreneurial success.

In 1982, right after I was let go from my big secure job with the American Crane Company, I wanted to get back into an area of manufacturing type of equipment which could be handled on a more local basis with less travel. There are twelve thousand machine shops in Southern California. I approached the Decaussin family on allowing me to sell their machines for a six-percent commission. They agreed, and after ninety days I had sold my first Fadal Machining center. Incidentally, the odd name FADAL stands for Francis, Adrian, David, and Larry, the father and his three sons. The company at that time was producing three machines per month and had trouble finding homes for them. My commission on that first machine was only $3,000 because the machines sold for $50,000 back then. I had worked for three months for $3,000, and my monthly gasoline, telephone, and auto expenses totalled about $1,000 per month. You can see that something had to give.

Well, here is what gave. I made twenty calls each day, and when I reviewed them at night I assigned each a number based on a one through ten rating system. A ten was a hot prospect to buy within thirty days. What emerged were some interesting numbers. Exactly ten percent of the people I cold-called were talking about buying sometime that year. At the end of a five-day week I had called on one hundred people, of which ten were talking. Those who were talking were rated above a five. Those who were more serious were rated between seven and ten. I would see the seven-to-ten rated prospects once a week until they bought. I would see anyone between five and seven once every other week until they bought. These compounded numbers snowballed. In the second week, there were ten more talking. At the end of three months I had 120 good prospects of closing within the year. The eventual numbers that prevailed over an eight-year period were that ten percent of the 120 good prospects were closed in one month. I could sell twelve machines per month if I continued the number of calls every day. This had held true for eight years, which I would say is a good track record.

Early on I recognized what I did well. I knocked on a lot of doors. Only later on did I begin to sharpen and refine my sales skills. There is a saying that in any field, ninety percent of what you do accounts for ten percent of the results and that only ten percent of what you do accounts for ninety percent of the results. I have recognized this to be generally true, though perhaps not the exact percentages. Imagine what you could do if you could identify what that ten percent is which accounts for about ninety percent of your end results. (In independent sales, the end result is money.) If you recognized that ten percent, as elusive as it may be, and concentrated on making that ninety percent of what you occupy your time doing, you would give yourself a huge raise.

During 1988 I had given the factory such a huge backlog of business that they had to put their dealers on allotment. I had sixty-five machines sold, with customers waiting for delivery. If I had not sold another machine for a year, my income would still be $250,000. Many other salesmen in the industry were now gunning for me and my territory. I learned a few years later that dealers and salesmen from all over Southern California were contacting Fadal to see if they could get a piece of my very large territory. The Decaussin brothers were very loyal to our agreement and never changed the rules. Generally most companies would cut a salesman's territory if he began to make too much money. Fadal was and is an unlimited opportunity and is the most classic example of an American business success story in the past two decades. They put an American-built product right in front of Japan's face and took their market. It's about time, isn't it? I guess you could say that we remembered Pearl Harbor.

My entrepreneurial example, as well as Dan Diorio's, was a good example of entrepreneurial opportunities in sales. If you have thought about sales, I strongly recommend pursuing a career. I personally know of no other business that with very little investment (only time, phone, and a car), can produce this kind of income. I am sure that a $700,000 investment in one McDoncald's franchise would not produce the same amount of money for its owner.

If this entrepreneurial path sounds like it is for you and if you are already in sales working for someone, approach your employer as an independent with a higher commission structure. Since you will probably want to stay in the same industry, should your employer decline your request to change the deal and if you are sure that you are better than average and could earn more income if the deal were fairer, get your company's competitor on the phone. See who is out there who wants market share and is willing to operate on a true performance equals reward basis. Go for the throat! If you are in a field entirely unrelated to sales, take a look at sales opportunities that exist in your field. At least you will know something about it. Go to the newspapers and see who is advertising for a salesperson, then approach them on an independent basis. With the recession taking hold and business laying so many people off, with one simple correction they could bring those workers back. The correction is, you guessed it, more sales.

Everyone in the world is a salesman whether he or she realizes it or not. Everyone is selling someone something. The factory worker must sell his boss on the fact that he does a good job, a child must sell his mother on buying a toy. The art of persuasion is universal. We all possess the ability to develop into effective salespeople. After all, there are no college degrees in salesmanship, and most people who are in sales had failed at other careers. Sales is a last-stop career opportunity and is potentially the most rewarding if you are prepared to dedicate yourself one hundred percent.

Another interesting entrepreneurial opportunity is one of the nature that my neighbor is involved in. I will not mention his real name but will call him Paul. I met Paul one afternoon while driving out to monitor the progress of a home that I was building in the country. Anything ten miles away from a freeway, incidentally, is called "country" in California. Paul was just putting the finishing touches on his home, which dwarfed my six-thousand-square-foot Mediterranean significantly. He had constructed a very nice twelve-thousand-square-foot place that had an outbuilding I had thought was a stable. It turned out to be a five-thousand-square-foot garage. Paul waved me over to talk. He was a nice, unpretentious kind of guy who normally wore a Tshirt and jeans with suspenders. He was in his early sixties. He introduced himself, and his wife asked how our house was coming. I told her I thought it would be done on schedule. Then Paul asked, "What do you do for a living? It seems that I see you out here at midweek, early morning, midafternoon, and early evening. Don't you work for anybody?" I said, "No, I got that out of my system years ago." He smiled and said, "You, too, huh?" I told him that I owned a firearms manufacturing company and a machinery sales business and that I bought and sold things when the opportunities came around. He shook my hand vigorously and said, "Damn, it's good to meet another entrepreneur." I asked about his business. He was obviously doing well. He said, "Come into my garage. I'll show you what I like to do." He took me into his five-thousand-square-foot garage, which had tile floors and a complete drop ceiling with fluorescent lights throughout. As far as you could see were 1957 Chevrolets, in absolute mint condition, twenty-eight in all. Each car, I knew, was valued at around $27,000. I had recently read an article on vintage '57 Chevrolets. I then asked him if that was what he did as a profession, to collect and trade vintage cars. "No," he said, "I only collect 'em. I don't want to sell 'em." Then I asked the natural question: "Where do you find all of them, and how do you generate income to continue your hobby if you never sell them?" Then he told me about his three car lots around the area where he sold used cars. He said that every now and then a '57 would come in at an auction, and he would buy it sight unseen. Curious, I asked some probably naive questions about the used-car business, because although I knew nothing about it, I do know that in the machinery sales business we tend to refer to questionable salesmen as "used-car salesmen" in a derogatory sense. I was certainly not going to alienate my new friend and neighbor by telling of our tongue-in-cheek impression of used-car salesmen. Anyone who had built a home this nice and who had a nearly one-million-dollar car collection had my attention and respect, enough that I wanted to hear more about his business. I expressed my interest in learning of his car business, and this is what he outlined. He began by saying, "Well, you buy a car at an auction, maybe twelve years old for maybe eight hundred dollars." I asked where these auctions were. He said, "All over the place. Used dealers get notices about them two or three times a week." Then he continued to unfold the details of his profession. "I detail the car a little and put it up for sale at, say, $2800. I offer to carry the paper if the buyer is not credit-worthy, but he must give eight hundred dollars down, and I'll finance the two-thousand-dollar balance for twenty-four months." Then I asked about interest rates that he charged.

He said twenty-one percent, the same as Visa and Mastercard. Then I asked about bad paper and how many repos he had to do. He said it was surprisingly low. With one third down, people are normally a good risk, although they are sometimes late on their payments. Paul had a compassionate side to him. When the discussion was on repos of his cars, it seemed that my new-found friend the used-car magnate was an honest, sincere, compassionate person. My next question was the magic question: "How many cars do you sell each month?" He explained that he sold a car every day from each lot and that he carried an inventory of thirty-five cars total. Here is a man who has an inventory cost of paying a sales commission of $200 per car, which, as he pointed out, was modest compared to the profit. Each lot, by the way, was nothing more than a small dirt lot with a mobile home as an office. My perception of the used-car guy is getting better!

Now I'd like to tell about the Cocoa Lady and the impact that she had on me in my early entrepreneurial years. In early 1982 I read about a lady in Chicago who was referred to by her peers as the Cocoa Lady of the Chicago mercantile exchange. It seems that this lady became quite well known as being very accurate in predicting the direction of cocoa futures, and with her discipline of learning all she could on the subject, she began trading her own account to make a living. A lot of people look at a commodity speculation as a method of putting some capital at risk in the hope of wildly good profits, but the cocoa lady traded her account only, making her living not from commissions on the trade but from profits. This was a gutsy, knowledgeable woman indeed!

Commodity futures are a vehicle that can make tremendous profits as the result of super leverage. Although this vehicle sounds very glamorous, with great reward can also come great risk. Commodity futures carry that risk and are not for those with weak hearts.

After I had read of the Cocoa Lady in Chicago, I decided that I could effectively trade one commodity only, as this lady had done successfully for many years and had beaten the market. I was right. During 1982 I traded as many as fifteen copper contracts at one time and earned the same amount as I had made working full-time for my former employer, the American Crane Company. A copper futures contract works like this: the commodity, in this instance copper, is sold in lots, or very large contract batches. In copper you would buy a 25,000 pound futures contract for delivery of the particular commodity at some time in the future. Hence the name futures trading was given. A contract in copper could be purchased for delivery as far ahead as eighteen months. Generally, the farther away the delivery date, the higher the price. After all, you have a lot of time for prices to go up. In 1982 I would buy a 25,000 pound contract by putting only eight hundred dollars (called the margin) down. The price per pound during that time would be fifty-eight cents. In other words, I bought the right to buy the copper, 25,000 pounds at fifty-eight cents per pound, which would be delivered in three months. Unless you are a copper foundry, you do not intend to take delivery; you are simply betting that the price will go up and that you will sell your contract at a profit. This method is called a long position. You could also trade a short position if you thought the price would decline. With 25,000 pounds of copper as our example, every one-cent raise in the price per pound equalled a $250 profit. How is that for leverage? The limit that the price can go up or down in one day is called a day limit. In copper this limit was five cents per day; it could not go higher or lower than that limit. A five-cent increase equals a $1250 profit on 25,000 pounds. In 1982 there was about a fifteen-cent per pound trading range, as I recall, the low being fifty-five cents, the high seventy cents. At my peak I was controlling fifteen contracts. For every one-cent rise in the price I made $3750. I do remember a day limit up in which I got my five cent raise on fifteen contracts and made $18,750 in one day! This occupied my time while I was doing my *Green Sheet Equipment Journal* and getting between used equipment deals. This is not for everyone, and I would certainly not advise doing as I did unless you were absolutely devoted to learning everything there is to know about one commodity only and have the discipline to avoid trading on news reports and emotion. There are more losers than winners in futures trading; what makes you think you can beat the guys that have been in it for a long time? I believe that, if you do your research better or as well as those involved in the manufacture or the harvesting of the particular chosen commodity, you can beat the averages if you concentrate on one commodity only. This was a very profitable period of time, one that I'll always remember with amusement. During this period of time, most of my friends had discussed whether or not I should seek professional help. After all, was it normal to take out a second trust deed on your home to gamble in the commodities market while out of work? As it turned out, my friends were absolutely right: I was not normal. I was trading copper futures, publishing an equipment journal, and buying and selling used equipment as well as selling new equipment. I did all of this while all of them were going to work at nine and coming home at five. Well, to this day I thank God I am not normal. Eighty percent of the nation's population is "normal." Why in the world would you want to be just like the masses of wage earners who are mediocre when you have the opportunity to be spectacular?

Now let me tell you about my inspiration to venture into commodities trading. As I said, I had read an article in a business publication about the Cocoa Lady of Chicago. It seems that this woman had toiled as a clerk at a downtown pharmacy near the mercantile exchange. Each day she would listen to the stories that some of her customers would tell as they came through her store. Almost always she would hear about spectacular amounts of money made on different trades each day. One day she was given her two-week notice that the pharmacy had been sold to a larger chain and that they would be staffing it with their own people. Thus she was headed for the unemployment lines. What was interesting about this woman was that she was determined to rely on no one but herself. Up to this point in her life it seems she had several disappointments, each of which was the result of allowing others to steer her ship. She had divorced the father of her three children after a six-year marriage because her husband had trouble holding down a job but would not allow her to work out of the home out of his own pride. After her divorce she was hired as a retail clerk by the owners of the small downtown pharmacy. She was a model employee who could be relied upon to open and close the store on most days and who was trustworthy in handling cash and in making deposits for the owners. This dedication was now down the drain due to an event beyond her control. The Cocoa Lady was interesting indeed in that she at that point in her life vowed never again to put herself in a position of dependence on anyone. She knew that she would be dependent on unemployment benefits for a while and perhaps on medical aid for her children, but in the back of her head she knew that she would never be working for someone again. If her new realm of friends wanted to rely on her, she would do her best not to be a disappointment, but she would never let anyone steer her ship again.

While collecting unemployment, the Cocoa Lady would spend afternoons at the library reading about cocoa production as well as its places of origin, markets it was sold to, and every single variable that might affect this one commodity. She sent for information on technical data of cocoa trading from the brokerage houses around the exchange. She had ten-year charts, five-year charts, two-year charts, and six-month charts that illustrated every price movement of cocoa for a decade.

During her study periods she recalled a well-dressed man who had come into the pharmacy on occasion. He was not like most of the other high-roller types who talked excessively about things that made little sense to her at the time. He was a kind, quiet gentleman who would buy a package of gum, and while he paid, she recalled that it was always she who would engage him in conversation. She would ask about his day's trading and if he had had a profitable day. She remembered that his reply would generally be very calm and composed, and she had the feeling that although he was an intelligent man, he kept his intelligence to himself. She imagined that he was not a trader on the floor of the exchange but instead a local businessman who had brokers trading his accounts. While this man occupied her thoughts during some of her cocoa study, she visualized him becoming an advisor or a confidant in her new direction in life, trading cocoa futures. Whether the Cocoa Lady knew it or not, she was on a successful path to her new career. She was already visualizing her mastermind alliance association with a person whom she felt certain could add some value to her pursuit. She also visualized her children living in a better, safer neighborhood than the tenement project they lived in now. She occupied her thought process with her newfound goals of achievement and success as a trader and prevented any negative thoughts from entering her mind.

After several months of collecting unemployment and studying for her new career goals, she decided to put together a model portfolio of trades. She illustrated a beginning cash position of $25,000, and within 120 days her account model was valued at $72,000. With this model in hand, she sought out a way of obtaininng initial funds to put her plan into action. After speaking to almost everyone that she knew, including her former employer, it looked like a dead-end street. She had also learned by talking with various brokerage houses that most wanted to see at least $100,000 in liquid assets, i.e. cash, before they would even trade an account for her. In spite of all the bad news, she persisted.

One day the Cocoa Lady was walking home from a brokerage house where she had stopped to pick up a copy of the most recent cocoa production report, even though she had not been able to establish an account. She stopped in at the pharmacy where she had worked to pick up some candy for her children. As she stood in line, a familiar voice from the person behind her asked, "What have you been doing with yourself lately?" She turned to respond to the man's question, and to her surprise she was engaged in conversation with the man that she had visualized becoming a part of her mastermind alliance. "Oh," she said,

"It is nice to see you again." She began to outline her career goal. After the exchange of phone numbers, the man asked to see the model portfolio that she had compiled. He wanted to show it to the broker who traded his accounts.

A couple of weeks passed, and the woman had assumed that there was not a lot of interest from her friend about the cocoa futures business until she got a call from him. He told her that he had presented her model portfolio to his broker and that the broker believed it was a luck situation. He asked her if she would mind putting together another model based on another 120-day period. She replied that she would be happy to do so although now she must begin looking for a full-time job since her unemployment benefits had almost run out. She said she felt that she had wasted a lot of time educating herself in a field that she truly loved, and now reality was setting in and she had to produce income. The man asked her to stop by his office the next day.

As she travelled across town on the bus the next morning, she could not help but wonder why he wanted her to come over to his office address. She knew that he was a businessman, but she did not know what he did for a living. She imagined that perhaps he was going to offer her an office clerical type of job since she had mentioned that she needed work.

Upon her arrival at the address given to her, she was surprised to see that the building was all law offices. She travelled up to the given suite number and entered. The receptionist asked her to be seated while she summoned the man. He came out, shook hands with the Cocoa Lady, and invited her back to his office.

Sitting in her new friend's lavish office, she realized that the very intelligent man was a corporate attorney and a partner in the law firm. He also invested quite heavily in commodities. He proposed a deal. He outlined to her that if she would trade his personal account through the broker that he used, she would receive thirty percent of any profit made within the trading period of 120 days. She would have absolute discretionary trading access to his account to instruct his broker of what trades to make and when to make them. He set a capital limit of fifty thousand dollars for her to play with.

At the end of her 120 day period, the results were impressive. The fifty-thousand-dollar account was now worth $100,000. He kept his agreement and wrote her a check for fifteen thousand dollars, which was far more than she would have made in 120 days as a store clerk. She wondered what he had planned for her now that she had proven herself. As it turned out, her new mastermind associate thought enough of her ability not only to loan her beginning capital but also to loan her money to purchase her own seat on the exchange. Now he never had to consult a broker who made commissions on trades and who possibly would give bad advice, for he had under his wing a woman who made her entire living based on one commodity, and he wanted her to do the same for him.

The example of my mentor in the futures business is a true story, one that I will always remember. Of course she has no idea of the influence that she had on me when I was reading about her success. I had always wondered why she chose cocoa. As it turned out, she had seen her children enjoy cocoa as well as chocolate candy for so many years that she believed it was a commodity that she had a close tie to.

In closer examination of the Cocoa Lady, let us see some of the success traits that she employed.

1. Total utilization of her time

2. Finding and soliciting the help of a mastermind partner

3. Searching for all information on her subject

4. Objective evaluation of that information

5. Her motives were basic and sincere. Her survival instinct of bettering her children's living condition made her feel good about herself and her achievements. It gave her a sense of high self-esteem.

6. She had to succeed since she devoted her attention to study of ways to achieve her new goals. She had nowhere to go but up.

7. She never gave up. Even in the face of adversity, she never threw in the towel. If she had taken a job out of desperation, it would only have occupied time until she put her plan into action. She was destined to succeed at her goal.

Another example of entrepreneurial success at its best is one that most people have heard of. This time I refer to the well-known Amway Corporation and its founders, Rich Devoss and Jay Van

Andle.

The Amway Corporation was founded on direct marketing priciples that would allow a person to earn exactly what he or she was worth in the sales and marketing field. The company has given countless numbers of people open-door opportunities to accumulate the amount of income they desire. Each of its salespeople has the opportunity of receiving overrides on others whom they bring into the business and train well to produce results. This is an organization that warrants further consideration if you are unsure of what field of endeavor to pursue. Here is what I have found.

1. It is an opportunity available to anyone.
2. It offers unlimited income potential.
3. Like anything else, you must work hard and diligently to do well.
4. It does take contingency planning as any venture would take.
5. They have a basic plan that has proven successful, but you will also need to adapt some of your own creativity.
6. You have virtually no credit risk. They are a very highly credit-rated company which pays its bills. You collect cash when a sale is made, and they pay their overrides like clockwork.
7. You have unlimited access to professionals who would be happy to become a part of your mastermind alliance.

Sales of any product or service generally have a large percentage of people making a small amount of money while a small percentage of people make a large amount of money. Amway sales are no different. However, if you feel you have what it takes to be in the top ten percent of a sales field, you will do nicely in this endeavor.

Another example of a friend of mine who accumulated a lot of wealth by applying the basic principles that you are holding in your hand is a gentleman by the name of Tony Maglica.

I met Tony for the first time back in about 1970. He was in the screw machine business. For those who do not find that term familiar, I'll explain. A screw machine is a turning machine that has the capability of doing high-volume production of round machine parts. Some of the parts that are produced by screw machines are ammunition cases for the military, which is what Mr. Maglica was manufacturing when we met in 1970. He had a long-run contract to supply ammunition cases during the Vietnam War. Other items that are produced on screw machines include nuts and bolts, pipe fixtures, small screws, and virtually anything round, including a variety of automotive parts.

When the contracts for ammunition cases began to wind down, Tony began to look for a proprietary product to manufacture and sell. While running jobs for the government had given him a fair amount of income, it was hard to control his own destiny when he made a part that was only a part in a total component that someone else controlled. If the person in control of the completed product did not do an excellent job of running his affairs, he would soon find the need for the parts nonexistent. Tony was always the type of guy that wanted to have absolute control of his destiny, leaving nothing to chance.

At the end of the ammunitions contracts, Tony became interested in the possibility of building a very high-quality flashlight that would be entirely machined on his automatic screw machines from a solid piece of aircraft aluminum alloy material. Until now most flashlights were viewed as simply cases in which to store batteries but were not really considered a vital quality component of producing a light beam where needed. Most flashlight cases were made of metalstamped sheet metal or of molded plastic. None had a suggested retail price of even twenty-five dollars; most sold for two or three dollars. The first to accept the idea of quality machined flashlights was a group of people who had to rely on their equipment more than most. Police departments around the world began to buy in great numbers, and military personnel followed. Soon the retail stores and mass merchants like K-Mart, Wal-Mart, Sears, and virtually all general merchandise stores began to sell his flashlights in great numbers. After a few years, Tony expanded his product line to include not only D-cell flashlights but also the smaller C-cells and AA-cells. Soon there was a Mag Lite™ for virtually any purpose or person imaginable. Doctors used the very small AA-cell mini Mags due to their size and reliability. Pilots used C-cells, D-cells, and AA-cells. Within a few short years, Mag Lite became a household word synonymous with quality and good value.

It did not take long, however, for foreign competition to attempt to infringe on patents that Tony had. After several years in court and seventeen million dollars in legal fees, he was awarded an injunction against foreign manufacturers' dumping similar products on the U.S. market. Mr. Maglica is certainly a self-made person. He immigrated to the U.S. with hope for a better life, visualized a tremendous opportunity, grasped that opportunity, and applied all of the principles available in this book to achieve his goals.

It is important to give credit to a principle that Mr. Maglica used well. That is the mastermind alliance principle. He was astute enough to draw upon experts in every field that would pertain to his personal endeavor and to keep those people happy to be a part of his achievement. A person who was instrumental in the success of Mag Lite is my longtime friend Don Keller, and this example would not be complete without mentioning Mr. Keller's contribution to the flashlight industry as a whole.

It is interesting that although my friend Mr. Maglica has achieved huge monetary success from the quality flashlight market as a result of applying the absolute basic principles contained in this book, my friend Mr. Keller was actually the very first person ever to conceive the idea of an aluminum machined quality flashlight. Mr. Keller attempted to put his thought into practice in the early '70s when he formed a company called Kel-Lite Industries. Kel-Lite was the very first aluminum quality flashlight, and Mr. Keller promoted it well but made some business mistakes along the way, eventually losing control of his company. He then joined the alliance of Mr. Maglica. Mr. Maglica was very fortunate to have Mr. Keller within his mastermind group for many years for his great contribution to the development of markets for the Mag Lite quality product line. However, Mr. Keller failed to control his own destiny, and eventually Mr. Maglica and he had a parting of ways, and the tremendous contribution that he had made to the company that he did not control had no monetary value to him anymore. This happens more than most people realize; without a good plan and without good contingency plans, there will be no success.

Thoughts only equal things when they are well conceived, well planned, and well executed. Without a plan and ultimate execution of that plan, a thought equals nothing of value except a memory to the thinker. I consider Mr. Keller and Mr. Maglica part of my mastermind alliance, as I have extracted things from them important to my success, and I have benefited by learning from them.

The Ultimate Entrepreneurs of All Time Award, in my opinion, must go to a group of people which has a very low profile but who took adversity and turned it into gold and in many situations literally turned trash into gold. My hat is off to those, mostly Jewish immigrants and their families, who were not offered employment when they arrived on our shores many decades ago. This group of entrepreneurs endured some of the hardest of times and in spite of their adverse situations prospered by collecting throw-away items that people no longer found useful and finding uses for them or their component parts. You now must know that I am referring to the junk men.

In the United States there are about twelve hundred scrap metal processors. These are businesses that collect scrap metal of all kinds, separate it into batches of like kind, and resell it to the steel and metal foundries that must have it to produce new metals.

During the early part of the century these immigrant entrepreneurs went out each day either to buy or haul away at no charge discarded items that had metal content, such as old ice boxes, carts, automobiles that no longer ran, engine blocks, radios, etc. Then they would take them to a lot, or sometimes their homes, where they would separate the different types of metals. The copper went into one pile, the steel into another. For copper they could get perhaps five cents per pound; for the steel perhaps five dollars per ton. It took a lot of steel to make a living back then; however, these businessmen knew value and knew how to buy their inventory. Their philosophy today is not much different than it was at the turn of the century, and that is the following: if you do not waste anything, you will never need anything. Waste is something that was intolerable to the scrap metal entrepreneurs; after all, people's discards that they traded in were considered waste to most of society, but they were the scrap dealer's livelihood. Today many scrap businesses are being run by the grandsons and greatgrandsons of the founding entrepreneurs who recognized the value of an education. Many of those running the family businesses today are lawyers, doctors, and well-educated people with at least four-year degrees. The unattractive junkyards of the past are now ecological processing sites. Many of their operators are PhD's. Most of these unattractive facilities spawned success of a magnitude that most cannot comprehend.

One example that comes to mind is that of a family in Northern California. I first met them while working for the American Crane Company. This family bought a lot of equipment from us to process the scrap metal that was derived from their ship-wrecking business in Richmond, California. This family company as well as others would buy surplus U.S. Navy ships at a bid price of perhaps ten dollars per ton. Well, the ship would weigh perhaps forty thousand tons, and their outlay would be $400,000. Ferrous scrap sold to the steel mills for perhaps sixty-five dollars per ton. The processor would have the job of torch-cutting the heavy ship's hull and deck into small enough pieces to fit into the furnaces of the steel mills. Some of the scrap would be fed by crane into huge hydraulic shearing machines that would apply clamping pressure. Then their guillotine blades would come down with thousands of tons of force, cutting the scrap into small pieces. The yield on a ship could be enormous considering that many tons of copper and brass were bought for perhaps ten dollars per ton and would go for over a dollar per pound, more than two thousand dollars per ton. Also extracted from the ships were all useable items. Most scrap processors that handle shipwrecking also have marine parts stores in coastal communities where they sell off all useable marine parts, including engines, compasses, and navigational equipment. I would guess that a ship might yield three or four million dollars in profit.

The scrap metal processors are a tremendously loyal group of people whom you can trust and confide in. They have seen it all in business, are excellent character judges, and expect respect and fair dealing from everyone who does business with them. God help you if you cross one of them or attempt to defraud them.

This entrepreneurial segment of society is a good example of prosperity in the face of apparent failure. If you have an opportunity to become acquainted with a scrap processor, I would recommend doing so. They have something valuable to share with every would-be entrepreneur. I would certainly seek one as a member of my mastermind alliance.

What is also interesting about the scrap metal processors is that they do something very basic, that is, tear things apart, sell off the components that once comprised the total sum of the complete product, and do that at a price that is higher in value than the finished good. It is not very often that you have a chance to view progress in reverse and at a profit.

Supply and demand is something that plays a

key role in the scrap business plan. In 1981, for example, I had the pleasure of escorting Mr. Katsanos, president of the Elisius Shipbuilding Company of Greece around the country to view some of the locations where our American Cranes were being used for ship-wrecking. During that period of time there were too many oil tankers in the world, and the Elisius Shipbuilding Company saw more value in tearing apart sometimes not very old tankers and selling them at scrap value to the steel mills simply because there were too many of them in the world. Ironically enough, several years after that they were backlogged with orders to produce new supertankers. What if a guy bought options to purchase these vessels at a time in the future for their scrap value then and sat on them until the demand came back around? Oh well, as you will see before you have finished reading, there is opportunity on every corner. The key is to recognize it and to formulate your plan to capitalize on it.

The recycling industry has unlimited growth potential, and I would strongly recommend that anyone consider this business, either as a broker selling into the paper or steel mills or as a peddler selling into the scrap processor's yard. It is, however, a commodity type of business and does offer the potential of great rewards with little investment. If this industry is of interest, go talk to your local scrap man. Chances are he will become a member of your mastermind alliance.

The pawnbrokerage business as a whole is probably one of the most profitable businesses to start from scratch to realize almost immediate cash flow. It can be started for as little as $25,000.

It is said that America would not have been discovered if not for the pawnbroker who lent the queen money for her jewels so that she could bankroll Columbus's adventure. Pawnbrokers serve a real and legitimate purpose in society. They lend money to those who might not be able to obtain it from more conventional sources. Granted, the cost to a borrower will be more, but whom else could a lot of people rely upon to give them money right away? As a member of the National Pawnbrokers Association and several state associations, I perceive the pawn industry to be comprised of honest, hard-working proprietors of small businesses who are extremely astute students of economics.

Generally pawnbrokers are governed by state as to the interest rates that can be charged for their loans. However, yields are normally boosted by structuring what was once a loan on a particular piece of collateral into an option or a repurchase agreement. Under a simple interest-rate loan, if the item being pawned were worth two hundred dollars, the pawnbroker would loan probably about twenty percent of its value. This small ratio assures him that you will return to pick it up and give him his money back. Under a simple rule of fifteen percent annually, he would receive only six dollars per year on his forty-dollar loan. However, by actually buying your merchandise and agreeing to sell it back to you at a time in the future, he can sell it back at whatever you and he agree on, plus storage fees for that period of time.

Pawnbrokers can generally produce returns of six to twelve percent per month depending on their mode of operation. By putting out $25,000 at loan, a pawnbroker can make between fifteen hundred and three thousand dollars a month. This is a very attractive alternative to doing the unspeakable thing of working for someone.

If you would like more descriptive information on starting a pawnbrokerage, you can contact the National Pawnbrokers Association at 600 S. Federal St. Ste. 40, Chicago, IL 60605 and request information on purchasing the publication called *Doing Business Under the Balls* by Patricia Taylor. This is a very complete and comprehensive guide to starting your own business, and it covers every conceivable detail.

A lot of times the best opportunities are in areas that most people will not have anything to do with. Take our entrepreneurs in the scrap metal business. Most of us do not want to get our hands that dirty, but as my many friends in that industry have shown for three generations, the dirt does wash off, and their industry has survived all economic events. The pawnbrokerage business has for some people been interpreted as a sleazy, loan-sharking type of operation. This is not the case. Yes, the rates are high, but the money is there when needed when banks will not talk to people. It is interesting to see the items that my friends at Beverly Pawn in Beverly Hills, California, are taking in pawn. They include a Rolls Royce, a Mercedes, and airplanes. These are items that the well-to-do segment of society had to give up only for a short period in order to obtain cash when needed and when they were unable or afraid to talk to their banks about loans. It is also interesting to note that there is now a large, publicly traded company called Cash America that is acquiring large numbers of pawn shops. At last count they had 171 store locations. Their trading symbol on the New York Stock Exchange is Cash Am if you would like to buy some stock. As you can see, a lot of opportunities were passed up by most Americans because of their unglamorous nature. A lot of us wanted to become attorneys or engineers; we certainly did not want to have to rely on our tenacity and entrpreneurial skills because most of us had none. Well, as the examples of these two basic industries illustrate, the dirt washes off, and the integrity of the entrepreneur is intact. I've truly enjoyed social and business relationships with these two industries for over a decade. If you can befriend your local scrap dealer or pawnbroker, I would urge you to do so. The advice he or she offers may be valuable, and he or she might be interested in becoming a member of your mastermind alliance.

I'd like to point out before closing this chapter that the failure that we will examine is my own. In the mid-1970s I began a flashlight manufacturing business. I wanted to produce a product rather than work at the machine shop I had been in since leaving high school. I had developed a trade as a machinist and had dutifully punched my time card every day for over nine years. This was a place to start; however, it was too similar to standing in line at the fat lady's window, with the exception that I had something to do with my hands.

In my flashlight business I constructed a high-precision, quality aluminum case flashlight that was very popular with law enforcement and others that needed better than average quality lighting tools. Here I was able to apply my trade as a machinist as well as other knowledge that I had gained in the manufacturing arena.

In my flashlight operation I utilized what I considered adequate production methods. Although I knew nothing about business, I was (I thought) above-average in the production arena, and, being young and dumb, I believed that this alone would carry me to success. Whenever someone would begin to sell me on higher production methods that would take a capital investment, I would shut their suggestions out and never give them the benefit of consideration. I was suffering from what I've recognized as I matured as a terminal case of tunnel vision. I had blinders on and was not open-minded enough to evaluate better production methods. As I look back I recognize also that I suffered from the intimidation factor, that factor that can strike so many of us and which is best described as the inability or lack of desire to implement something that one knows nothing about. After all, those high-production, six-spindle turning machines were things I knew nothing about, and I felt very comfortable manufacturing our flashlight bodies on singlespindle turning machines even though the other machines could produce six times the production at about the same cost after the investment in the equipment.

As you can conclude, my worst enemy in my first business venture was myself. I failed to listen to those who wanted to become part of my masterminding alliance; I was the only member of my mastermind group, which proved to be a very lonely organization and the ultimate contributing factor to the demise of my first attempt at a proprietary product. Every mistake that could be made in business I made. I even made some that the most seasoned professionals had never heard of. You might say that I was the inventor of many new ways to fail in business. In fact, I could have written a book entitled *1,000 New and Interesting Ways to Fail*. I certainly had the credentials to do so.

What I think of in reflecting back on those years is my friend Mr. Maglica, who recognized my shortcomings and set up after my demise to flood the market with the Mag Lite. Mr. Maglica deserved his tremendous success. He had forsight in recruiting the best mastermind alliance, and he had the enormous production capability of supplying the fifty million-dollar-per-year market that purchases his product.

It was after my tremendous failure that I decided to get into sales. I was certain that I could not get into too much trouble by talking, or so I thought. I knew something about equipment, so I went to work as regional sales manager for the American Crane Company. Although it was an adjustment, going to work for somebody meant that I had lots of security, right? Wrong!

It is interesting to see the number of salesmen who chose their particular profession only after failing at other things. Of all the sales professionals I know, both men and women, none of them intended to become salespeople. There is no degree in salesmanship. You can study marketing, but that is not sales. No college in the country or in the world teaches sales. The art of persuasion is an art of its own. It is probably the most powerful tool in the universe. If you have ever had to persuade someone of something, you have attempted to master the art of persuasion. In fact, the world's opportunities belong to those who are persuasive. This is the only field that offers unlimited earning potential without a formal education. It is very possible to land on your feet after failure, especially in sales.

In 1988 I was confronted with the biggest challenge of my life. I had always wanted to manufacture a proprietary product and market it. I had failed miserably in my first attempt in the mid-1970s flashlight phenomenon and had resorted to entrepreneuring it in the sales arena. I had made income in the top one percent of the nation's income levels, but I wanted to rectify my failure in manufacturing. This sounds very dangerous, doesn't it? I thought it was extremely dangerous myself until I evaluated my situation and the knowledge I had gained through my failures. I asked myself why I wanted to take a chance when my sales business had done so well. Why did I want to tread away from what had apparently been my calling? Well, I knew of an opportunity that could be very profitable in the manufacturing of a certain type of firearms, and its production methods could be very profitable. The only thing in the way was a company that had monopolized that particular market segment for over twenty years. Now you must be saying that, wow, this is really sounding dangerous, right? Wrong. The reason this was such an opportunity was because of the company's dominance for over twenty years without competition. Remember our theory of being at the top of the ladder? Well, this company was there and had been for over twenty years. Needless to say, complacency was setting in, and with the slightest nudge they could topple down the other side to make room for the new kid.

This decision, as with any decision that I make today, was not a guess; it was not an assumption, and it left no element to chance. It was a calculated decision that has become for me a process of evaluating the risk versus the reward and then isolating the risk component and methodically evaluating each and every risk obstacle component, then devising a method of eliminating those elements.

Every person whom I talked to about my venture thought I was crazy for attempting to knock off the big guy that had dominated this market for so long. I chose the right alliance in the beginning by associating with a gentleman who became my fifty-fifty partner in the firearms business. He brought to the table the expertise that was needed to get production underway, while I applied my talent of stealing market share. We were successful at wresting a major chunk of this particular market share away from the big guy on the block in less than three years, and conservatively I would estimate our dominance of over sixty percent of the market within the next two years. The successful combination of different talents has worked well here and testifies to the power of the mastermind alliance coupled with limitless thinking. "Can't" should not be in your vocabulary.

I have one more success example to relate before I end this chapter. This one is a mother-daughter team in downtown Los Angeles. The mother had been laid off from her factory job, and her daughter was attending community college classes in the late afternoon. This team of innovators saw an opportunity in preparing sandwiches that were exceptionally good and priced just a little more than cafeteria and lunchtruck food. The mother and daughter team would go into highrise buildings downtown and stop in every office within the building just before break or lunch times with their baskets of homemade delicacies. They were well received by everyone. Both mother and daughter were very personable people, and everyone enjoyed spending his or her money with well-deserving, energetic entrepreneurs.

The novelty caught on fast, and before long the two ladies had gotten agreements from building owners throughout the downtown area to allow them and only them to enter their buildings for the sale of food. Each building owner was paid a concession fee for allowing the women to operate within the building.

Within a year the women had to hire other independent contractors to cover the enormous number of offices in the downtown area. Each of the independent operators became his or her entrepreneurial boss. The mother-daughter team had developed into a lucrative franchise operation. Until the unfortunate (or fortunate) event of the mother's being laid off from her job, she had never heard the word "'franchise.'' After her brief period of standing in the unemployment line, she had decided as I had that she could do better for herself.

In every adverse situation there is the opportunity for a great reward. Sometimes it takes some searching to find it, but it is there to be found.

What is evidenced by the sheer numbers of unemployed or underemployed people in the U.S. is that we will become a society of entrepreneurs, and the shift in that direction is becoming more apparent as unemployment benefits run out and as public aid policies slim down. It is the basic human instinct for survival that is spawning the entrepreneurial spirit in America today. Most of us are not quitters. Remember that we have those special loved ones who are dependent on us. We do it for them and in the same token do it for ourselves. Some of us will slip through the cracks, but most of us will survive and will hopefully contribute by offering opportunity to others.

THINGS TO REMEMBER
1. There is nothing wrong with failure.
2. There is something wrong with giving up.
3. While being out of work is a humbling experience, you may want to consider seriously a career change to an entirely different field.
4. No career should be considered to be beneath you. Remember it is you who are out of work. There is nothing wrong with this because it was probably not under your control. Forget about prestigious titles. I can introduce you to a pawnbroker who earns $400,000 per year in his pawn shop. So what if you are no longer an $85,000 per year bank president! Titles mean absolutely nothing, and in fact in today's corporate climate a title will quite certainly put you on the endangered species list.
5. Attempt to master the art of persuasion regardless of whether you decide to pursue a career in sales. This will benefit you in all aspects of any career. This applies to presidents and CEO's as well. Remember they must convince shareholders of their company that they are doing a good job. The art of persuasion applies to every aspect of life. In today's litigation-happy society, civil suits heard by jury have nothing to do with who was right or wrong but with whether the defendant's counsel or the plaintiff's counsel has the ability to persuade a jury of his way of thinking.
6. Note that all of the success examples that I have used had failures that preceded their successes. Some of them had many failures, but none of our examples gave up. They may have given up

temporarily and gone to work for someone while regrouping, but eventually they all came back to draw upon the strengths they had learned from the failure.

7. Channel all strengths toward positive results only. This means no negative thinking.

8. Don't be afraid to get your hands dirty in an occupation you had previously thought beneath you. You can always wash your hands.

9. If you are fortunate to catch the ear of a financial backer in your new venture, be totally honest and do not burn bridges. If this is a personal ability that you don't have, you should look around you and take note that perhaps this is why you are continually failing. You must develop the total honesty approach to business and life. If you do not, you are only cheating yourself.

GETTING BACK TO BASICS: SMALL IS BETTER

9

Large enterprise has been the goal of most companies' directors for many years. For nearly a century the mentality was "the bigger the better." During the '80s, leveraged buyouts created mammoth enterprises that attempted to operate under very heavy debt loads. Who benefited? It was certainly not the holders of junk bonds, that popular issue of high-interest debt that investors bought like there was no tomorrow to finance these acquisitions. If anyone benefited, the brokers of this debt instrument were the only ones. Leveraged buyouts were kind of like our scrap dealer who bought the finished product only to sell off the parts that brought a far better yield than the product's value itself. As long as there is demand for those component parts, the seller keeps selling them for profit. In the case of the leveraged buyouts of the '80s, the component parts were corporations that had assets which could be liquidated at a profit while being acquired through creative debt. During the '80s this was the rule, not the exception. What was sold along with the corporate parts were millions of jobs. This is when the erosion of the middle class began. Now, in the '90s we are seeing the proverbial circle return to corporate America. They wonder where the buyers for their goods have gone. Well, you don't have to be a rocket scientist to know that if there is no middle class, you will not sell goods in any appreciable quantity. During the '80s corporate America began to dismantle its own basic infrastructure and sell off the pieces to show a better bottom line for the time being. Long-range strategy was out the window, top-level management thought only quarter-to-quarter and watched its stock's value soar as the return on their assets climbed. Eventually there were no more assets to liquidate, and a lot of folks were out of work. Concentrating on the remaining core businesses that were left, many large companies found that there were no buyers for their goods. What these highly educated, Harvard business graduates were successful in achieving was the dismantling of Henry Ford's creation, the middle class. While Ford had little education himself, he had a lot of common sense and the ability to draw upon his mastermind alliance of the most educated people in the world and to consider their input. It was Ford who developed the five-dollar day. This was a pay scale he found that would enable everyone working for him to be able to afford to buy an automobile, thus perpetually fueling economic growth for his company. The more cars they sold, the more workers he had to hire and so on.

Eventually, the Ford pay scale was viewed by most as a barometer for pay. Thus, middle-class America was born. These were not rich people or poor people but a middle class that could afford to purchase household goods that were produced in record amounts for a growing population. This philosophy in reverse was the path of corporate leaders in the '80s, and it appears it has come full circle in the '90s. Our well-educated corporate leaders orchestrated the party of the '80s only to be confronted with the hangover of the '90s.

I must apologize to those of you well-educated executives who had nothing to do with this turn of events. If it sounds like I am belittling a good education, I am not really doing so, although the extent of my own education is only to the eleventh grade. I did not graduate from high school because I had to provide financially for my family. I never felt that I had missed anything. I did attend community college part-time for a few years to study business law and economics, but most of my education came from reading volumes and volumes of business publications and from practical experience. One of the better lessons in business is simply to recognize what you do not know.

Now with idled workers, demand for those companies' products has dried up. Banks are failing due to record numbers of bad real estate loans. Real estate in many areas is becoming worth less than is owed on it, and our banking system is strapped with nonperforming loans because of unemployment or underemployment. The nation's insurers that have been given the responsibility of managing some private pension funds of your employers attended the cocktail party of the '80s as well. As it appears in the '90s, they drank until they could no longer move. The hangover they face today is real and has contributed largely to the purchase of junk bonds as well as overvalued real estate. You may be shocked to see how your pension fund, if you have one, has been invested.

In short, folks, America is in a bad situation. The national debt is absurd. Twenty-five percent of all taxes collected from every taxpayer goes to paying the interest on the amount of money that the country owes. You may say, "Okay, so what? So we have a lot of debt, it hasn't seemed to affect my surroundings." Well, have you ever wondered who it is we owe all this money? The national debt is not created simply by printing more money and having our elected politicians drop into a box a hand-written IOU which will someday be paid. U.S. treasury bills are sold at auction at discounts from their face value which yield generally modest interest rates. These have the appearance of very safe security, but by what are they backed? That's right, the full strength of the U.S. government. Big deal. That and a dime may buy a cup of coffee. These debt issues of the U.S. government are backed by the full strength of the U.S. taxpayer. What if the U.S. taxpayer is unemployed? What if a small business is out of business? Who is the taxpayer now? The larger burden will begin to shift to the fewer people who are still employed or in business, and this tax burden will be far greater than before. Who is buying this enormous amount of T-bills? A lot of foreign governments and foreign companies find our obligations attractive, especially Japan. Right this minute if the foreign countries that hold our debt were to ask for redemption and to receive their money, it would bankrupt the U.S. Treasury. We are fortunate that maturity dates vary significantly and penalties apply for early redemption, because if these guys called our IOU we would have to pack it in or develop another creative method of financing our government. How about junk bonds? Perhaps our politicians could learn how to acquire capital by rubbing shoulders with the guys who attempted to eradicate the middle class. How about selling off the White House to a Japanese limited real estate investment trust and then leasing it back? Look at the tax advantage. The Japanese could benefit by receiving the depreciation allowance, and the U.S. government could deduct its entire lease payment as a cost of operation. I would bet that when George Washington slept at the nation's capital, he could not have imagined how much debt we would eventually have and that he would be cutting a check to the Japanese just to stay there!

Well, enough doom and gloom. You can read about that stuff in the newspaper or watch it on T.V. You bought my book, I presume, to learn how to make money without answering to anyone and perhaps to get back to basic winning principles. You can see, however, that you are probably not alone in hard times. Our government is a comfortable companion in misery, although our politicians are not paid on performance. There is no disgrace in a hard-working individual who is honest having financial difficulty. After all, the largest corporations in America are, too, as well as our government, our banks, and our insurance companies. It is shameful, in my opinion, though, to dwell on the problem and to fail to carry on in a positive manner.

Banks are a good example of sympathy seeking, as are savings and loans. When they hit a snag due to nonperforming loans that were a result of the cocktail party of the '80s, depositors were safely insured either by the Federal Deposit Insurance Corporation or by the Federal Savings and Loan Insurance Corporation. Depositors trusted these institutions to take diligent care of their money, and our government insurance fund was to insure their safety to the tune of $100,000 per depositor. It sounds pretty safe, but it has turned out to be kind of like asking the homeless for a loan. At this writing, both guarantee funds are without cash. The failing institutions are being teamed up with stronger banks to take over some of their obligation for mismanagement. How is this for penalizing the successful? What happens when the FDIC and the FSLIC have depleted their reserves and when all the strong banks have taken on as much debt from the failed banks as they can shoulder? Well, those seekers of guaranteed safety for their savings accounts will then receive their funds from the taxpayers. You may ask if it is fair for the individual who may not have any savings at all but who still has a job to have to replenish the lost deposit due to the mismanagement of a bank or savings and loan that he has never set foot in. Or you may wonder why someone who has opted to shoulder a little more risk by buying the stock of an American company and thereby becoming an owner of that company but who has no guarantee for the safety of his principal, why should this person as a taxpayer have to contribute to the safety-seeker whose bank or savings and loan has failed him? I personally think that government should steer clear of banking with the exception of providing some basic regulations. Let the crybaby whose bank failed shoulder the risk. That is a true free enterprise system.

I believe that our country would benefit tremendously if business people ran it. This may sound contradictory after my criticism of corporate America during the '80s, but there is a lot of business talent out there that has had the experience of many decades of running huge enterprises. I think that Congress as well would benefit from being run by well-tenured business leaders. Just think of a presidential team of Lee Iococca and Ross Perot. Congress would become America's board of directors, and the country would be run for profit. Under this example we would stand a far better chance of economic survival. If either Ross Perot and Lee Iococca or Warren Buffet and Sam Walton ran for office, they would get my vote. How in the world did the American people get suckered into giving their votes based on charisma and popularity polls?

In earlier chapters we talked about how we are

perceived by others as well as our images of ourselves. Well, imagine how vain our politicians must be to make cash offers to bail out other countries from their economic problems when we do not have the money ourselves. It's kind of like a loan from the homeless, isn't it? Is this fiscal responsibility? Aren't you glad that your entrepreneurial path will add to the prosperity and quite possibly the salvation of our country?

As economic woes are staggering our safe, secure companies as well as our nation, it will be up to each one of us as individuals to bear the responsibility of turning the tide. By becoming an entrepreneur, you are becoming part of an historical event that will probably reshape our nation's thinking. Big is no longer the name of the game. Small and profitable is the way the game will be played in the future.

THE HEART-MIND RELATIONSHIP

10

Thinking is something that all of us have the ability to do. As discussed earlier, we can all control the thoughts that enter our minds. These thoughts can be conceived as well as believed by the subconscious mind, whether or not they are true. When subconscious suggestion is used in repetitive thought, what is really colored white may now appear to be green if you have convinced yourself of it. Once the mind has been convinced of the path you are taking in life or business, the physical aspects that it takes to accomplish those goals and the details that it takes to put your plan into motion come almost automatically, almost like a programmed robot doing what it takes to achieve the end result. In other words, thoughts do become things.

We have discussed the importance of believing what we let enter our thoughts. It's an absolute that every tangible thing that we see around us today was at one time just someone's idea. This alone illustrates that the principle of thoughts being things is without a doubt a very, very powerful tool. Best of all, this tool is available and within the grasp of absolutely everyone, though there are some obstacles.

First of all, it is important to note that what the mind can conceive and believe, it can also achieve. What is a key element here? The absolute key is believing! It will take a long time to convince the subconscious mind of something the mind believes to be untrue. The subconscious resistance to the untruth that the thought carries and the argument with the mind to reject what is thought to be an untrue statement will occupy your thoughts most of the time. However, when you add your heartfelt emotion to this equation, you have overcome the biggest obstacle of belief and argument in the thought machine. When you speak from the heart you are believed by the mind. It is also very hard to deceive the two. A good example is that of a man and a woman in love. When confronted with logical facts about one another that are not to the hearts' liking, the minds tend to shut out the reliable information that they have received.

Your heart is a powerful tool. Salespeople that excel above the rest are speaking from the heart in their persuasive arguments to prospective buyers. When speaking from the heart it is perceived by the individual that you are speaking to that you absolutely believe what you are saying, so there is no doubt in your prospect's mind that what you are saying is fact. When speaking from the heart you are giving it your all. Win, lose, or draw, you have gained the respect of everyone in your audience because you have spoken what you believe in your heart, and this is an emotion. Every human being has emotion and can display emotion. When something is presented or pursued with belief and emotion, you will win.

Have you ever heard the expression in the sport of boxing that "he has a lot of heart?" Well, what is meant here is that the guy with a lot of heart is giving over one hundred percent. In spite of the fact that his opponent may have superior skills, the guy with the heart is always respected. A lot of times in boxing the guy with more heart and less skill will win simply because he applied more pressure and refused to give up to the superior skills of his opponent, while eventually the superior skills of his opponent started to subside as he was worn down. The guy with the heart wanted the win more and was driven from within by emotion. The ideal combination for a fighter, however, is to have developed superior skills through discipline, planning, and contingency planning and to possess a lot of heart.

The heart-mind relationship is important to your success or failure. When introducing your positive thoughts to your thinking process, you must be truthful and honest with yourself. Does it matter if your goal is somewhat high and unbelievable? Not at all! This is not an untruth entering your mind; it is a goal that you visualize meeting, and there is absolutely no reason not to achieve it. You should aim for the moon, and if you fall short of the accomplishment, you will come far closer than if you were content with a lower aspiration and had succumbed to mediocrity. You want to become better than average, far better!

Whatever comes from your heart is an emotion, and it will be answered with emotion from the person who will be affected in the transaction or deal. In our boxers example the emotion or "heart" that the fighter gives are punches, and they are answered with punches. A lot of times decisions are based on emotion. It is interesting to see how emotional decisions are made and how conclusions are drawn. A decision in itself is the expression of an emotional response to a demand that is made upon the maker of the decision to act.

Depression is an emotional form, but depression is not a disease that is contracted but is rather a mental state that we create. How do we create this mental state of being? You got it: by our thoughts. Who can control the thoughts that the subconscious mind receives? Right again: you can. You are the master and the only accountable source that allows information into your thoughts and decides which information the subconscious will decide to believe as truth. The key here is to occupy your thoughts with only beneficial material that will be of value to you in your entrepreneurial endeavor. Do not allow time for any other thoughts. Remember that while the competition is home watching TV, you have the same time that they do, but you will choose to use yours a little more wisely.

A practical example that comes to mind of the heartfelt emotion turned into action to overcome deficiencies in other areas of expertise is an event that took place in Sacramento, California, in August of 1988. My older daughter Lori had introduced me to her new boyfriend Tony Lopez while we were visiting her at school. When my wife asked our daughter what Tony did for a living, Lori replied that Tony worked for Murdoch Brick Company and was also a part-time professional boxer in the junior lightweight division. You can imagine the thoughts that went through my head at the time. As we began to know Tony, though, we began to like him. If he were not successful as a boxer, he could have made it as a salesman. I respected the tremendous discipline that he had showed in his stringent training. He had been boxing since he was just ten years old, and his father and older brother were his motivators for pursuing the sport, as they had both boxed professionally as well.

One day it was announced that Tony had gotten a chance to fight for the International Boxing Federation's world championship in the junior lightweight division. He was to square off against a very seasoned champion named Rocky Lockridge. Lockridge, as I recall, had forty-three professional fights and zero losses. Thirty-four of his fights were won by knockouts. Tony had a respectable record of twenty-three fights with one loss and seventeen wins by kockout. The ranking world sanctioning bodies had never ranked Tony in the top ten, and it is unusual to see an unranked fighter get a chance at a world title. Lockridge had gone on television and had said, "Tony Lopez is not even a contender, but I will give him his chance because he is young and hungry. However, I will knock him out." That day in August we were at ringside, as was national television. Tony entered the ring and had the strong support of the crowd estimated at thirteen thousand in attendance. Tony's purse was thirty thousand dolars, twenty-five thousand more than he had ever made before. Lockridge got $200,000, which was not his best pay. He viewed Tony as easy work. He was wrong. Tony came out like a tiger. I could tell who had the heart, although in round eight a big right hook from Lockridge to Tony's left temple made Tony hit the canvas harder that anyone I had ever seen go down. I was yelling for him to stay down, while my wife was screaming for him to get up. Well, he heard my wife and got up to hang on through the remainder of the eighth round. When he came out in the ninth there were no ill effects from the previous round. He went after Lockridge and administered pain that resulted in sixty-three stitches to Lockridge's face. Lockridge has not fought since, and we got a new world champion that day. The fighter who wanted it more in his heart prevailed. The world title that had been etched on Tony's subconscious mind since he was ten years old was now his. The people of Sacramento, who had been hearing this little Mexican kid with green eyes talk of becoming a world champion since the fifth grade, saw a thought become a thing that day in 1988.

THE DIFFERENCE BETWEEN A JOB AND A CAREER

11

As I reflect back on my young and dumb years, I recall interpreting a job as the menial task I toiled with just to survive. A career, of course, I interpreted as the longer objective of lifelong commitment to a noble field that must be fulfilled perhaps for humanity itself. Well, as I grew and saw full circle the way that things really are, it became very apparent that this interpretation could not be further from the truth.

The jobs that were viewed by most as only a means to survive at the time are a key component to the whole business picture in America. While most Americans of my generation (baby boomers) had attitude problems in demeaning those who carried out the tasks of assembly-line work, our Japanese counterparts were praising their assembly workers and making them a bigger part of the total picture. Do you recall the quality control methods of yesteryear, when there were almost as many supervisors as there were workers and when American companies had established quality control departments that would check the accuracy or quality of each operation when it was already too late? Well, those supervisory personnel were layers of fat in our competitive industries. The Japanese, on the other hand, taught the workers who were performing the particular jobs or operations to inspect and insure their own quality before the component got further down the line. Guess whose principles work better? The results began flooding our ports: Hondas, Datsuns, Sonys, and Mitsubishis, all superior products.

We now see that the only difference between a job and a career is how the individual views his position. It sounds rather derogatory to refer to someone as a career hamburger flipper, doesn't it? What about Dave Thomas of Wendy's Hamburger chains? He flipped burgers, viewing it as a career and a business opportunity, and has done very well. What about Carl Karcher, president of Carl's Jr. Hamburgers? He was quite a grill man himself, as was Ray Kroc, founder of McDonalds, who also sold milkshake blenders for a time. It is pretty apparent that only attitude makes the difference between a job and a career.

There is a woman by the name of Carmen who works for my firearms manufacturing company. Carmen has personally assembled triggers on all of the more than 110,000 firearms that we have sold. Our triggers are the best functioning in the world for our specific firearm; Carmen sees to it that they are. I am very thankful that Carmen views her work with the best possible attitude, and she has a career running our trigger assembly as long as I am in the firearms business. She is as important a component to our operation as my partner and is more so than our attorney. Whose job is merely a job and not a career? Everyone should examine his or her definition of jobs and careers. Anyone who adds value to my product has a career with me as my partner and mastermind alliance member. Anyone who costs me money in professional expenses is expendable and a burden to my business. To me, he or she is the one toiling at a job. I hope that a lot of professional can see themselves in this picture and possibly adjust their attitudes and perception of those trying to survive with the tools at their disposal.

Another example of a job versus a career is illustrated by my gardener, Fortino. We used to have a lawn service take care of our lawn. All they did was mow the lawn. Would they ever think of replacing a sprinkler that they broke? Of course not. They only mowed and edged. We ran across an older gentleman named Fortino who was doing labor work on landscaping for a few others in the neighborhood. Everyone I spoke to said that Fortino was the guy for gardening, and they were right. He treats our grounds as if they were his own. If he is driving by and sees a weed, even if it is not the day we are scheduled to have our lawn mowed, he will stop and pull that weed. Fortino has no set time to work on our yards; he simply gets the job done without looking at his watch. He is a professional in every sense of the word. He is in charge of our place's being well-kept, and his pride in his work is apparent.

We are fortunate to have surrounded ourselves with good people, people who are the best at what they do and who are a part of our mastermind alliance. I hope that we are able to keep them happy working for us and that they do not decide to become their own entrepreneurs, except Fortino, who is one. Carmen, our trigger lady, works for our company, and her trouble-free triggers are very important to us. She could be charging us a fixed cost per trigger as an entrepreneur, and by becoming extremely efficient could certainly make more than we are paying her. Does this give you any ideas?

There are virtually limitless possibilities for you to change careers and land on the track running, perhaps even doing the same thing you are doing now but for more money and with freedom to explore more opportunities. Today a lot of companies are viewing independent contracting as a better method of getting a job done at a fixed cost without the burdens of benefits, unions, and absenteeism. A graphic example of this that comes to mind is a friend of mine who had worked as a senior design engineer for a large company that manufactured plastic flexible pipe and hose. This friend was furloughed after sixteen years of dedicated service. He asked my advice for career paths that he should pursue. He had always thought of himself as a salesman type. Well, I know a salesman or a trainable candidate when I see one, and this guy did not fit the bill, which is not to say he did not have the social graces or appearance necessary to become a salesman. He was simply not a good listener, only a talker. He did not have the ability to hear the other person; consequently, when the prospect was ready to buy, he would just keep talking until he had talked his way right out of a sale. You could possibly even overlook this bad trait and rationalize that in spite of that he was trainable, but the problem was that this fellow had been in a senior engineer's position for so long that he was not going to change easily. He would resist change every step of the way while arguing about why the teacher's method was right and his method was not right. This guy was a very structured thinker. He was structured to think in logical terms. Well, in sales or the art of persuasion, there is no black or white, and sometimes decisions are made for a reason that an engineer or a mathematician could not comprehend because it does not appear to make sense. An astute master of persuasion listens for the soft spots and begins to push the exact buttons necessary to accomplish the end result, and more often than not two plus two does not equal four. Unless my friend was able to abandon his logic and to devote an ear to the aspects of human nature, he would never make it in sales. However, there was no denying that he was a top-flight design engineer in the plastics field. My suggestion to him was to have some business cards printed up and to approach all of the companies that he knew could use his services as a consultant on a per-job basis. Right away the company that had just let him go needed his services for about fifteen hours per week, and now he was earning what he was worth. He started his enterprise over three years ago and is currently doing design engineering work for companies all over the U.S. and has a waiting list of customers. He is earning about thirty-five dollars an hour, about fifteen dollars an hour more than he made working for his former secure company. What my friend found, as all entrepreneurs do, is that security is money. There is no getting around this simple axiom!

A lot of times a company lets someone go simply because the company no longer needs the person's full-time services. If approached on a contract basis of receiving the person's talent only when needed at a fixed cost or on a per-job basis, they will be most willing to give the person a try in an entrepreneurial role.

Another good example of the same humble beginning is that of a fellow by the name of Danny. He was a service man for what was once the largest machine tool company in the U.S. This giant growth company eventually met its demise as the result of all the typical mismanagement reasons: unbridled spending when things were good, no discipline in maintaining a cash reserve, officers' and directors' salaries that were too high, and mainly the inability to recognize shifts in trends relating to market conditions. They had no abibility in the bob and weave department.

Danny was furloughed with nowhere to go after eight years of service. The machine tool business was suffering from the recession in that industry, and Danny was not alone in his situation. There were many other service technicians who were in the same boat. What Danny recognized early on was that although new machinery was not selling well, there were thousands of machines of the type that he serviced in use at machine shops in California in particular. He saw the need for those aging machines that would require repair, and he jumped on that demand. He established his service company and never looked back. The benefits his customers gained were the same good service but for less money than was charged them previously when the customer was paying for the tremendous mismanagement of Danny's former company. The customers' bills no longer reflected the costs of providing management with Mercedes 560's or $100,000 cocktail parties. The customer was now billed only for a value-added service to their equipment and no more. Danny had recognized through his initial misfortune of losing a job, the opportunity that existed, and had capitalized on it in a big way. Almost immediately he was earning twice what he had made working at that great secure company whose payroll checks barely squeaked by the bank each week. Danny may very well be driving his own Mercedes today and rightfully so. After all, he earned it!

THINGS TO REMEMBER

1. If you view your job as a profession and strive to be the best at what you do, your job is no longer just a job but is a career.

2. Your attitude towards the duty you perform is the only difference between a job and a career.

3. There is no shame in not having a higher education. Don't carry this around with you as an excuse not to excel.

4. Do what you do with pride, always trying to better yourself in every way.

5. Look around at all of the entrepreneurial opportunities that are within your field of expertise.

6. If you have recently become unemployed, what do you have to lose by trying your hand at entrepreneurship? Nothing!

LANDING ON YOUR FEET

KNOWING YOUR LIMITS

12

As discussed earlier, we are not always the way that others perceive us to be. Many times we are not even the way that we perceive ourselves to be. A lot of us go around having quite a bit of bad luck and difficulty in the pursuit of happiness and harmony. Well, believe it or not, luck plays a very miniscule part in whether or not a person accomplishes his goals and objectives. Your success will be achieved solely by a well-thought-out, calculated plan that is free of flaws. The fewer the flaws, the higher the probability of your success.

To achieve the flawless plan, we must first recognize that no human being is flawless. With that in mind, and with all successes being the product of human beings, can in fact the plans we make be free of flaws? Probably not. However, do our plans have to be absolutely free of defects in their compositions? Not really. All they have to be is good enough to sell and as good as we can make them based on the resources available.

You can get very involved and detailed in

preparing a plan of direction. A very simple plan like crossing the street may be carried out without a flaw; however, a plan to cross the street in exactly 3.5 seconds and against cross traffic at high noon could have a flaw or two in it and will likely take a more detailed look to achieve.

You must recognize that no one is perfect. Although we all know of someone who would have us believe that he or she is perfect, we must recognize that not even you, the expert at your profession, have one hundred percent of the problem solving capability that it takes to put together a successful enterprise free of flaws. You will most definitely seek ouside consultation in your pursuit of a plan. Do not go around banging your head against the wall because your plans seem to be blowing up in your face; let an outsider in to handle the things that you recognize are your shortcomings. If you are not good at something, then get someone who is, and quit bucking the success formula. You could very well be your own worst enemy just as I was with my first business failure. On the other hand, if we recognize our shortcomings, we can prepare and deal with them accordingly. Remember, you are the orchestra leader and not the musician; knowing your limits is an absolutely basic necessity for your prosperity. The sooner you recognize this, the sooner you will see things take shape without catastrophe.

That you are doing something wrong is pretty apparent when turmoil seems to surround everything you do. When there are always adverse things happening that you feel are the results of someone else and when you feel that you are simply the victim of all this terrible stuff, look in the mirror, my friend, because the fault most certainly is your own.

A graphic example of deficiencies that go unnoticed is that of an acquaintance of ours whose driving record is full of accidents from when she was between twenty-five and forty years old. This lady was in an accident at least once a month, including some minor ones. Once she totalled a new Mercury that had less than five hundred miles on it. Another time she was driving a new Chevy truck home from the car lot when she broadsided another truck. What was interesting and apparent early on to everyone around her was that every time she told the story of the accidents, it was always the other guy's fault. I must ask you: do you smell a fish here? I guess our friend's example is kind of like that of the commercial airline pilot who has flown 747's for twenty-five years and has never had even so much as a close call. Then you have Captain Bob who has not only successfully avoided ten mid-air collisions and is proud of the fact, but he has also walked away from a couple of ground crashes as well, none of which was his fault. Now, given the choice of riding with the first captain or with Bob, would a prudent person choose Bob? Hell, no!

Our poor friend went around believing she was never at fault and that her driving was absolutely great. After all, it was always the other fellow who crept into the intersection just before his light turned green. While she might have been right on that point, we all know that you must drive defensively to avoid other drivers. However, knowing this lady, she probably saw the other guy creep into the intersection but had a yellow light and time to spare and thought that, by God, it was her right to go through that intersection, and she was not going to let the jerk out there until it was his turn. The lesson that our friend was oblivious to most of her life is that there is a price to be paid for principle. In this lady's case, she wrecked cars, one after another. But, by gosh, it wasn't her fault, and she was always in the right each and every time. Well, in this graphic example, it doesn't take a rocket scientist to see that principle and who is right are nothing if the consequences are the hospital or the morgue.

This attitude in business is going to put major restrictions and limitations on you. If you are a closedminded person and are not open to listening and extracting value from the comments of others, you had better change because your self-imposed limitations will not allow you to progress naturally, and your creativity will be zero as well. If you have achieved any successes so far in your life with a closed-minded attitude, those successes are surely limited by yourself and left mainly to that miniscule element of luck. To become a limitless person and in business enterprise, there are no hard heads allowed.

Chances are that a great deal of people can see themselves in this portrayal. If you are of this nature, it is not too late. You can change for the better to prosper with limitless thinking.

THINGS TO REMEMBER

1. Analyze yourself objectively. (Sometimes this is hard to do.)

2. Confront your limitations by recognizing them.

3. Do not be intimidated by someone who knows more than you do.

4. Develop a clear, concise plan for recruiting help in the areas to which you are limited.

5. Get rid of the proud peacock syndrome. It has no place in business.

6. Do not stick with principle to the detriment of progress. Principle and a dime won't buy you a cup of coffee in business.

ENTREPRENEURIAL OPPORTUNITIES

13

Opportunity to make money as an entrepreneur is abundant. We've examined examples of my personal friends who have become successful at a variety of enterprises. Their successes are not accidental or lucky breaks. Each of these people created a method of capitalizing on an opportunity that presented itself through either his own creative thinking or someone else's. Each of these people, however, had enough desire to pursue the opportunity until it paid off.

It's important to realize that simply recognizing an opportunity and wanting success do not equal money. To equal a cash equivalent from the enterprise, you will be called upon to put forth a plan, and, most importantly, the action that it takes to achieve the end result. You might say that any successful venture has three components: first, the thought or idea; second, the plan that has been well thought out many times and which has many contingencies; and third, action. In almost every failure to succeed at something the biggest culprit has been in the action department. It could be said that you may not need the first component, the thought or idea. (After all, it may have been someone else's and not your own.) However, the other two components are absolute necessities.

The very best plans or ideas are a moot issue unless acted on. After clearly defining what is expected of you to become successful at your enterprise, let us now examine some legitimate opportunities that virutally anyone could capitalize on.

First, let's look at sales opportunities. This is a field of great opportunity with little downside risk. The opportunity of sales, however, does take every single element of our success formula plus one not mentioned. The unmentioned component is tenacity. You must be ready and able to handle rejection as well as intimidation. You must have very thick skin, and this is something that you can develop from experience. When you feel that one approach to a potential buyer is not working for you, do not go so far into your presentation that you have given him an ultimatum of a decision that might not be in your favor. Always leave yourself an opening to pursue the presentation in another light that may be more pertinent to your customer's way of thinking, even if he or she is wrong. After all, you want to do a good job of presenting your facts as you know them to be true; however, every one of us has run into that hard-headed and sometimes obnoxious customer who has an ego the size of the Grand Canyon and who thinks he is always right on every issue. In dealing with guys like this, I always like to concede to them regardless of how far out in left field they are. I have found it best to agree with how right they are, feed their egos, and get down the road with the commission check. After all, guys like this are not applying the very basic success principle of evaluating input and are too caught up in themselves to be objective, so their bad decisions could be viewed as your reward if handled properly.

When making available your services as an independent commissioned salesman, you may want to stay within the field that you are already familiar with, or you may want to pursue a career in an entirely different field. If you decide to stay within your industry, you may want to approach your current employer to negotiate an agreement at a percentage to be paid on performance. A lot of companies like this idea because it is a fixed cost and it only costs if an order is brought in. In this scenario, though, think about whether the commission should be paid upon order, upon shipment, or upon payment. This should be a very important issue to bring up because depending on your cash position your mode of payment will be a very important subject. Should your pay be based upon collection, you should receive more for your sales commission because you have shouldered some credit risk yourself. Another very important question to ask when negotiating your deal is, if the commission is paid upon shipment or when the customer pays his bill, how long will it be before either of these events happens? In the machinery business, sometimes deliveries can be as far away as six months to a year. Can your financial situation accommodate this cash flow method? These are all very valid concerns for you to consider when you negotiate your deal. The most common method and the fairest is for a commission to be paid on delivery, not when the supply source is paid, but this is also dependent on the percentage of commission. For example, you may have the choice between a twelve-percent commission to be paid on the receipt of payment to your supply source that you represent and a ten-percent commission paid on delivery with no credit risk on your part. Depending on the cash position that you are in, you may like the additional two percent, especially if you are sure that the customer will pay your source within thirty days. After all, twenty-four percent a year is far better than you would earn at the bank.

An interesting thing about the sales game is that although it is an intangible asset, there is certainly a dollar value after you have developed a territory. This dollar value can be determined only in the relationship between your net income and your cost of doing business. As an example, let's say you earn $100,000 per year in commissions. Let's also assume that your out of pocket costs of operating, including car, airfare, gasoline, insurance, and phone is $16,000 per year or sixteen percent of your gross commission income. You have a net income of $84,000, which is slightly more than five times your investment of $16,000. I know of almost no other investment that will return five times in one year. When you consider what type of value to place on a sales territory (should you ever decide to sell it), you may want to consult the *Wall Street Journal* to see how many times a company's earnings most major public companies are selling for. A very conservative PE ratio (percentage of earning ratio) at this writing is nine. In other words, a very conservative purchase price for a lot of companies is nine times what a year's earnings may be. With this in mind, it would not be entirely out of the question based on the nine times multiplier to value your business at $756,000 (nine times $84,000). A McDonald's franchise will cost its owner a minimum of one million dollars per location; however, the owners would be extremely fortunate to pull $100,000 a year out of the location. What is the point of comparison? Well, the McDonald's franchise just laid a one-million-dollar investment on the line. Whether it is cash or financed, it is still one million dollars invested to earn $100,000. The guy with the McDonald's gets a one tenth per year return on his investment, while our independent salesman gets a five hundred percent return on his $16,000 investment and has an income almost equivalent to the McDonald's guy who went into debt a million dollars to earn what our salesman will earn. Is it becoming clear why I favor sales as an independent as a career path?

What are the intangible aspects of the sales business? Well, unlike our McDonald's guy who may have some equipment that has a dollar value, the independent saleperson's only real asset is himself and his ability. When planning to buy a sales territory, a buyer should take special notice of the fact that although Joe made an excellent living selling his wares in the territory, there is no guarantee that the buyer will do as well. Also, what does Joe plan on doing after getting out of the business? Taking on another line perhaps, and competing with the buyer in the same territory. The best way of winding down or realizing the final value of your independent sales organization when you are ready to retire is to make sure that you have expanded with the help of other capable salesmen that will eventually take over and write you a check once a month to stay home.

Another asset that should clearly be mentioned that you as an independent salesperson will have, is the good name and name recognition of the product, goods, or services that you sell. It is important that you associate yourself with an absolutely reliable source. There is nothing worse than a salesman spending a major amount of valuable time explaining to a customer why there is a problem; this simply takes time away from the next deal.

For those of you who are planning on employing this career change, I would give this advice: if you are a seasoned professional with a client following built up over many years, you have a distinct advantage prior to approaching your employer on a better deal. Also put out some feelers to your competitors to see if they want to work a deal with you as an independent rep with unlimited potential. Should your gut instinct tell you that you can work a deal with one of your competitors that will net you a considerable increase in income, then approach your employer on the deal. At least you will have backup alternatives if needed.

In absolutely everything that you do, regardless of the career path that you choose, and even in your personal affairs, alternatives are a very important part of life. Never put yourself or, for that matter, allow anyone else to put you in a position of necessity with no alternative measures. This is not only a precarious place to be, but the person in that position may be a danger to himself and to others. Conversely, in most business dealings where sales are involved, you try to structure the deal to be as beneficial to all people related to the deal as possible. There are, of course, exceptions to this rule; if you are playing with the hardcore element you may be confronted with a decision to go for the throat.

Should you be in a position that dictates a complete career change in sales, here are some opportunities that could be yours for the asking, with almost no background at all on the subject. Mortgage brokering comes to mind as an excellent opportunity, especially in today's economic mess. With interest rates at their lowest levels in over two decades, the demand to refinance homes and other real estate is very high. Virtually any mortgage broker, if approached on a no-risk commission deal, would be happy to have business cards printed with your name on them as their representative.

If you are determined to stay in sales or

become involved in sales for the first time, just remember that there is a reason that the economy is in such bad shape, that reason? you guessed it, lack of sales!

Almost any industry in America today could benefit substantially from additional orders. You must develop a presentation to those companies that would benefit from your services and sell them on the idea of giving you a chance. So much for this type of sales, let's examine some others.

In almost every city in America swap meets and local flea markets are springing up one after another. These community stores are a very good place to rake in some extra cash. All you have to have is something to sell; find some things to sell. If this sounds like a statement that is being made without a lot of thought given the subject due to its simplicity, you are wrong. A lot of thought was given to the recommendation of this method of entrepreneurship, and if it sounds too simple, that's because it is that simple. You find something to sell, and you sell it! These swap meets and flea market locations, while unattractive in nature, are certainly more affordable merchandising arenas thaan the community boutique. My friend Dick Cepek, who has passed away, was very successful and began his business in the swap meet arena. Dick was a consummate entrepreneur well before the term became fashionable. In the early '70s, Dick began buying retread tires from various retread sources in Southern California, and he would load down the U-Haul trucks with all varieties and sizes and take them to the swap meet locations he and his family had throughout the state. His sales volume climbed beyond anyone's imagination, and soon Dick saw trends within the tire industry that compelled him to get on a plane and visit Singapore and other Asian countries that could economically produce specialty tires with his name on them. Those specialty tires seemed like modern miracles to the hundreds of thousands of off-road vehicle enthusiasts throughout the country. He had specially designed wheels that had straight flap-tread design for soft sand as well as nobby tires that more conventional off-road vehicles like Jeeps would require. Then came the ATC craze, and Cepek was there, eventually building his empire to over one million square feet of warehouse space to store his CEPEK brand tires. Of course, he became involved in a full line of offroad accessories as well, all of which were put into the DICK CEPEK off-road accessory catalogue that was mailed to hundreds of thousands of people each month. Dick was able to bypass conventional marketing techniques and to go directly to the consumer, which meant bigger profits for himself. Rather than going from manufacturer to wholesaler, wholesaler to dealer, and dealer to consumer, Dick Cepek did things unconventionally and was extremely successful. All of this from peddling recapped tires at swap meets! What does this tell you about humble beginnings? There is absolutely no disgrace in humble beginnings, and any preconceived image of yourself of something being beneath your ability is only a preconceived limitation that you've placed on yourself. Attitude, as you will find out in your new beginning, is a very large part of the battle.

Another opportunity that is apparent is that of our friendly scrap metal dealers. In virtually every major city in America there is a scrap metal processor recycling various types of metals to sell back to the metal mills and foundries to become new material again. These processors buy scrap material from peddlers who receive the material from manufacturing entities that cut metal parts and sell the remaining scrap. While there could be an investment in machinery as well as land to become a processor, not to mention the work it would take to get a major steel mill to buy from a new kid on the block, very little is needed to become a collector and peddler of scrap to the processors. Generally, you would approach companies that generate scrap aluminum, copper, brass, and steel, and offer them a fair price for their remnant materials. You would determine what to pay for their scrap by what the scrap processor is paying you, and the difference is your profit. Naturally a truck or a small fleet of trucks is needed, depending on how good you are in the persuasion department and on the accounts that you get.

If your resources permit an investment of twenty-five to fifty thousand dollars, you may want to consider opening a used-car lot. I know the stigma surrounding the used-car salesman; however, especially after meeting my new neighbor and examining his success in that business, I believe that above-average income can be achieved almost from the start. We are dealing with an economy that does not allow a lot of people the luxury of buying new cars. There are a number of vacant gas stations and other bare lots that could be ideal locations for car lots if zoning allows. A lot of this vacant property could be leased for a percentage of your sales on a month-to-month basis, just to make it produce some sort of revenue for the owner to pay property taxes.

In considering the used-car business, you would want to go around to the new car locations in your area and solicit their trade-ins that have a few too many miles on them for them to sell from their lot. The new-car dealers often do not want to market something with forty or fifty thousand miles on it because they are not set up to service makes other than their own. In some cases, if your art of persuasion is working well, you may be able to work consignment arrangements as well, thus reducing the amount of money you wrap up in inventory. As with any business, your capital is your life-blood, and whenever you can structure a deal with little out of pocket, even if you have the money, the better off you will be. Even if you have a cushion that you feel is adequate, remember, you are entering a business arena that is unfamiliar to you. Have you considered your mastermind alliance? Do you have a plan and a cash projection? Take the most pessimistic plan and cut its results in half. This should be your barometer for evaluating your initial cash projection and profits. Now that we've shot holes in your plan, if it still holds some water, there is a strong likelihood that you will succeed. But remember that in the beginning you want to approach every cash expenditure as though you are penniless. When you feel that you can barter rather than pay, barter.

I know that to a lot of mid- and upper-level executives who have found themselves out of work, the used-car business probably does not sound attractive. Let's look at it this way: you will continue to learn about people, even though you may have a lot more on the ball. It may be a humbling experience in the beginning, but you will be providing a needed service to a segment of society that needs what you offer; therefore, there is worth. I believe that the used car business has the potential to capitalize on an economic event that dictates its need as well as the opportunity of breeding new entrepreneurs. At this writing I am giving the used car business some serious thought myself. Another key aspect of starting this business we must talk about before getting off the subject is financing. Almost all used car buyers will need financing; therefore you will want to find a local bank or finance company that will take your paper. Generally the paper they will be buying will have a higher credit risk than that of a new car; therefore, they will receive higher interest rates (i.e. eighteen percent or more), but they love the higher credit risk, especially if the security is not too far overvalued. Example: a 1982 Ford retail blue book listing (what a lender will use to determine how much to loan) is, say, $3200, and the lender may want to see a twenty-five percent down payment, eight hundred dollars. Well, you probably bought the car wholesale from the new car lot for one thousand dollars and put a few dollars into it for clean-up and service. The customer gives you his eight hundred dollars down, and you receive the balance from the lender. You will want to develop a good working relationship with the lender or finance company, and from time to time the company may ask you for recourse on the deal; in other words, should the buyer default, you will make the loan good. There is nothing wrong with this on occasion due to the high profit potential of tripling your investment, after all if the buyer defaults, you or the lender pick up the car, and you can sell it again. Eventually, as your cash position builds, you will want to carry some of the financing yourself because of the lucrative rates you can earn and the ease with which you can remarket it should it become a problem loan. My hat is off to the used-car guys. I can now appreciate their business as I never did before.

Since we are dicussing used cars, we might as well discuss other things that are used. In any bad economic climate there are certain businesses that will flourish. Just like the used-car dealers of America, used-furniture dealers have great opportunity. At the beginning of the recession, it became apparent that with housing sales heading south, a lot of people were not buying new furniture as they had in the '80s. There are fewer households being started now due to later marriage ages, the direct result of a bad economy and of more demand being placed on the participants. Although the households that are being set up do need furniture, these households tend to consider used furniture if there is a significant difference in price. Like any business, used-furniture dealers need a source of supply. You could use conventional newspaper ads stating in bold type "We buy used furniture and appliances." Use the same publications to advertise them for sale. You could approach the local remaining new furniture stores and ask them for their help in letting their customers know that they have an outlet for their used furniture. Now that they have used you as a buyer for their customers' used furniture and appliances, they may well sell more new furniture because those customers can turn their old stuff into cash to use toward new purchases. Once you have located your sources of supply, all you have to do is find a warehouse. Keep in mind the same principles that applied to our car lot example. There is a lot of vacant real estate out there; strike your absolute best deal, using as little cash as possible.

Another good venture to consider for capitalizing on a bad economy is the pawn brokerage business. This business I have paid special attention to over the past few years because of the relationship between firearms and pawnbrokers. It is a market that the *Wall Street Journal* wrote about my exploiting aggressively to sell my firearms to and ultimately gaining major market share in our specific type of firearm. The pawnbroker adds legitimate value to our society: he loans money to a segment of society that for various reasons could not obtain money from other sources. He loans money on the spot with no credit requirements; he will loan on almost anything. The margins or amount that he loans will be only a fraction of the item's value, but this is his security. After all, if he lends ninety percent of an item's value, there is strong probability that the item will never be picked up and that he will sit on it for years before selling it, and he does not want to tie up his money for long unless the return is BIG. From state to state and area to area, a pawn broker's yield will vary, however, what I hear is returns of upwards of 50% a year. In other words with 50,000 dollars lent on pawn, you will produce income of 25,000 dollars per year.

In my opinion, business ventures like pawn-brokering are worth evaluating the risk-reward ratio and considering all avenues of obtaining cash to start a business like this and our used-car lot. I personally would even consider refinancing my residence if I needed to begin this type of business. After all, what is the risk? If a pawnshop yields over fifty percent a year and you borrow money through remortgage sources at 7.5%, you don't need a Ph.D. to see that there must be some money left over. Rather than going into all the details of what it takes to open a pawnbrokerage because it is far more detailed than any of the others and spotting value is so important due to the greaat variety of objects that are pawned, I will strongly recommend that in lieu of a mastermind alliance, there is one publication that is the only publication to my knowledge that outlines in every detail what it takes to start a pawnbrokerage. The author, Patricia Taylor, has many years and many stores under her belt, and in my opinion is the foremost authority on the subject. Her book, entitled *Business Under The Balls*, can be purchased by calling 818-334-1518. It is $59.95 and worth thousands of dollars more than that if you want to start a very lucrative business. She offers a thirty-day money-back guarantee as well. Her publication is very large, with step-by-step illustrations of every single aspect of the business, potential pitfalls, and sources for merchandise and evaluation. This investment is less than the cost of dinner for your mastermind alliance group and is hundreds of thousands of dollars cheaper than leaving your plans in this industry up to chance.

Thus far we have discussed sales-oriented and buy-sell businesses. Now it would be worth looking at the service type of business. These businesses often can be started with little capital and are attractive alternatives to working for a supposedly secure company. One service-related industry that I became familiar with through a friend that started it is the janitorial services business. This industry is open to anyone who wants to learn the trade. Some of the skills that you will need besides becoming knowledgeable of the technical aspects are your salesmanship or power of persuasion, which will be called upon even in the janitorial business; after all, you will have to find the users of your services as well as convince them to give you a try. They may currently be using someone else, and it is your challenge to convince them that they should use you over the other company. It is amazing how many times in every aspect of life and business we are called upon to become salespeople, and the janitorial service business is just one more. Generally this type of business takes little capital investment, perhaps four thousand dollars as a maximum. In every region of the country there are wholesale janitorial suppliers; these folks, in return for your business, will be happy to direct you to the right equipment to get started. This, like any business, has the potential of growth limited only to the entrepreneur's thinking. You will recognize that soon you will be contracting out your accounts to someone else working under you, and you will do what you do best: get more business. Should you decide to pursue this segment of the service industry, I would not overlook another segment of the janitorial service industry that goes hand in hand with it, and that is carpet cleaning. The people that I have done research on in this industry do home carpet cleaning as well as their regular janitorial routes; they claim that carpet cleaning is a very good source of revenue in addition to office buildings.

Another service business is that of a gentleman whom my wife recently contracted to clean windows and mirrors in our home four times per year. I had an opportunity to talk with this team of brothers who wash windows, and this is what I found. One of the two, the older brother, is about forty years old and has a four-year degree in business administration. However, due to severe cutbacks in business administration in the aerospace industry, his company no longer needed his expertise. Does this sound familiar? Within a short period of searching for something that suited his experience, he decided that he and his brother could become window washers par excellence. Keep in mind that this man has a respectable educational background but had never flown on his own. They charged us $180 (which I thought was a steal), and they did not only our home but our neighbors' the same day for the same price. If it was an equal split between the brothers, this would average each of their incomes based on only a twenty-day work month at $43,000 per year. This, to a lot of us, is not a lot of money; however, in view of unemployment it is a lot of money as well as an opportunity to build your own enterprise. Since the two brothers here are above average in intelligence, I would expect their business to flourish within three years and their incomes perhaps to triple, making the window-washing business a little more attractive to almost everyone reading this book.

Yet another service industry that takes little capital to begin is that of the auto detailer. The auto detailer of today is prepared to go to your place of business or your home and clean, wax, and polish your car for around fifty dollars. You will also receive extra good upholstery cleaning and generally as close to a new-looking car as possible. The detailing entrepreneur can do about four cars per day, depending on the travel distance. If he runs it himself, he has the opportunity to earn two hundred dollars per day, about what the window washers earn. However, by subcontracting the labor to others and paying an hourly rate of, say, eight dollars an hour, you could solicit more business and soon be on your way to earning good to great income from cleaning cars. This, like every other example, is limited only to your own creative thinking. The detailing business, I can see, would even have value to the new- or used-car dealer.

A business that I have not seen throughout the country but a demand that I recognize exists for the right entrepreneur, is mobile car washing. That's right, going directly to a remote area with a high-pressure water truck and washing cars. Why? Well, have you ever parked in an airport parking lot and come back from a three- or four-day trip? If so, you will know what I am about to suggest. I would have given fifteen dollars easily to know that my car would be washed the same day I was due to arrive so that I could at least see out my windshield for the trip home. There are a lot of ways to approach this business. One way would be to handle the payment throught the parking lot cashier who is already collecting money for the parking lot owner, let the owner in on the deal perhaps thirty percent, and have him cut you a check at the end of the month minus his thirty percent for allowing you to operate on his lot. In the same token, you have added value to his operation.

Since we are talking about service businesses, it would not be right to leave out the bridal service business. That's right, being a professional who takes care of the bridal details prior to the wedding. I met a lady doing just this who claims to be earning a net income of $150,000. I wish I knew more about the intricate details of such an operation; unfortunately, I do not. However, due to the lady's statement, I think that anyone interested in weddings might want to pursue it as a career rather than an objective.

Another service business that is worth mentioning is that of the model and talent agency. The experience of a friend of mine we will call Cheryl is a good example of what can be done in this field. Cheryl has been successful in providing trade show hostesses to various industries for their conventions and shows. These women look exceptionally congenial and almost perfect in every way and greet customers and attendees at these functions.

Cheryl was a model herself and had an entrepreneurial desire to do more within the same industry and to capitalize on the knowledge that she had already acquired. Although she had no formal education in business, it did not take long for her success to materialize after she pieced together her mastermind alliance group and formulated her plan. Shortly after following these basic necessities, she put her plan into action.

Cheryl essentially got between the models and their income, and she was extremely good at it. She organized to such a degree that many of the exhibitors at some of the largest trade shows in California called no one but Cheryl when it came time to hire talent with pretty faces.

Today I know of at least four very large trade shows that Cheryl's models work and no one else. Here is how she got started. She went around to each woman at every trade show that she targeted and asked them questions. With these answers she gained a lot of information as to what was lacking in each model's career as a trade show hostess. While there were the typical complaints like favoritism within the current agency that they were working for, there was one complaint that Cheryl heard more often than others. That complaint was that most of the models were not working often enough. With this argument in mind, Cheryl contacted each of the exhibitors that the models worked for and asked how each woman was doing and if they would like to have the assurance of getting the same models at each show, giving their clients exposure to the same person each year as well as eliminating the need to train a new girl each year on the products and procedure.

The going rate for the same model's services through Cheryl was now twenty percent higher than the other agencies' charges. The model's pay was ten percent less than the other agencies were paying. You are probably asking yourself why in the world anyone would pay twenty percent more for the same thing, and you would naturally wonder why the models would take ten percent less. Well, aside from Cheryl's employing every single topic covered in this book to achieve her end result, she added value to the service. The added value to the client was the guarantee of receiving the same totally trained, knowledgeable model at each show and giving the impression that this pretty, personable, knowledgeable girl was a part of the company. The benefit to the models worth forfeiting ten percent of their hard-earned money was that now they worked as much as twice the hours they had worked before, and they enjoyed the absolutely professional relationship with Cheryl inasmuch that her ground rules commanded absolute respect from client and model. Cheryl's operation is first class, and God help the model or client that steps past his or her boundaries.

What we have witnessed in viewing Cheryl's operation is exactly the same method that is used in most entrepreneurial dealings and excactly the same plan used in my very own first entrepreneurial deal when I profited from the silo transaction. Cheryl created an option.

She first asked questions and gathered needed information. With this information she extracted the major complaint that she believed could be overcome quite easily by simply approaching the source and getting a positive answer from the source that they would be interested in the same model at each show at a slightly higher rate. With this knowledge, she approached each model about working through her with the assurance that they would work more hours for slightly less hourly wage. What we've seen here was an option created that became a thirty-percent spread or commission for the option maker, Cheryl. Cheryl is truly an example of someone who made her own breaks and left nothing to the element of chance.

Today I can name at least five trade shows that Cheryl controls with no less than sixty models at each show. Each woman receives on average two hundred dollars per day, of which Cheryl receives sixty dollars. She also utilizes her same pool of modeling talent for photo assignments and other jobs.

Everyone that I have talked to in gathering information to write this book has encouraged me to give as many examples of entrepreneurial paths that are available to women as I can. With this in mind, I have paid special attention to women who have been thrown into adverse situations generally by circumstances that were out of their control. One of my valued critics, Mrs. Ruby Simpson, whose daughter Jennifer was given the job of editing my writing, has pointed out the importance of women with small children being given direction. With this in mind, I would like to illustrate the entrepreneurial opportunity that a young woman my wife knows employed to earn income to assist in a bad economic climate that her husband was thrown into.

My wife's acquaintance, whom we'll call Georgette, turned a hobby into a business when her husband was affected by the shake-out in the Southern California construction trade. Georgette enjoyed fashion art and had experimented with putting designs and sequins on women's clothing. She became very creative, using her imagination and going the extra yard in designing sequined arrangements that turned ordinary T-shirts or tops into magnificent pieces of fashion. Her designs were original and far better looking than any other similar fashions that my wife or I have seen at upscale boutiques in Palm Springs or Beverly Hills, and they sold for less than half the price. In Redlands, California, on every Thursday night you will find Georgette selling her art fashion from a street display on market night. Sometimes it is hard to get past the crowd to step in and say hello and place our order. According to my wife, Georgette has the most distinctive art fashion that she has ever seen and could be selling it for three times the money at any boutique in the country, and let me assure you that my wife has been to them all and knows what she is talking about on the subject.

Georgette began her business on the kitchen table with a glue gun and sequins that were bought at the local craft store. She was pretty much assured success when almost every friend that she showed them to wanted to buy one. This told her something. She then did her research, taking all the basic steps like every successful entrepreneur. She asked people what they liked and built upon that input. She then formulated her plan to market her works. With limited capital and still learning herself, she chose the most affordable method, the local street market as well as some flea markets. It is amazing what the cost of retail space will do for the price of a product. As mentioned, in an upscale boutique Georgette's fashion art would bring three times the money, but it would have to due to the cost of real estate. She brought real value to her family when it was needed, and her children are active in the enterprise as well. This in itself is success, just seeing the kids being involved in an enterprise that they show a great interest in at a young age. Georgette's business will be limited only to her imagination and persistence, and right now it appears that she has both in control and is clearly steering her own ship with the support of her husband and family. This is an enterprise that takes very little to start, but it does take what we have stressed all along, i.e. the idea, the plan, and the action.

Asphalt is something that almost every person in modern society sees almost every day of his or her life. Everywhere you look you are likely to see a pavement of some sort or another, from parking lots and streets to playgrounds and driveways. Sounds like a big market, doesn't it? Well, it did to an intuitive man that moved to California in 1963. This is a business that virtually anyone with little knowledge of the process can learn easily and with a minimal investment in materials and equipment, as Mr. Melvin Phillips found in the mid-60s.

As a teenager being raised in a poor neighborhood in a suburb of Los Angeles, I developed a friendship with some kids down the street whose father, I recognized much later in life, possessed most of the basic qualities necessary to achive financial freedom with no reliance on outside forces. Melvin Phillips had a seventh-grade education when he moved his wife, two sons, and daughter from New Castle, Indiana, to Baldwin

Park, California in 1963. His children and I attended the same schools and became good friends.

During this period of time, I perceived my parents as having more on the ball so to speak than Mr. Phillips; however, he was a nice, hardworking fellow who drove an old Studebaker pickup and did odd jobs and house painting for a living. As a youngster, I thought that this was not a real career or job and was proud to say that my dad worked as a welder for the Alhambra Foundry and that my mom was a typist for the California Department of Employment.

It was only as I grew older that I recognized the significant difference between Mr. Phillips and my own father. This difference, I would come to recognize, is what this book is all about, the difference between limited opportunity and opportunity that is limited only to your own imagination.

I remember when my friend Ron Phillips told me that his father was doing asphalt repair work and that that was why the old three-quarter ton Studebaker was so dirty all the time. The kids at the school yard where Mr. Phillips would drop off Ron and his brother Charles would always give them a hard time about that Studebaker truck being so dirty with asphalt and grease all over the outside of it.

Mr. Phillips applied the positive thought process better than anyone I had ever seen then or have ever seen today. He would drive his old truck over to the local rock quarry after dropping his kids off every morning and would load the truck up with almost a full ton of hot asphalt. With the old Studebaker dragging on the ground with shovels and hand rollers hanging off the sides, he would set out to find a customer that needed a parking lot repaired or possibly a new driveway installed. This approach obviously involved some risk because asphalt hardens like a rock in about eight hours, and Mr. Phillips had no prearranged job site lined up for its use. Mr. Phillips had not only to find a good prospect for his services, but he had to become a master salesman in order to persuade the prospective client to allow him to do the job immediately before the asphalt was no good. Mr. Phillips created a no-going-back demand on himself, and he did so intentionally because he knew that with no going back, he had to win that customer's trust, and it was reflected in his sales pitch. He put this same demand on himself every day of the week. Interestingly enough, each evening he returned home with not even a shovelful of asphalt left on his truck. The following day Mrs. Phillips would march down to the bank and deposit the receipts of the day before.

Mr. Phillips, as it turned out, learned how to operate and prosper out of necessity because perhaps he did not have any preconceived limitations that his thought process allowed in his mind. Each morning, he later told me, when sitting at the rock quarry getting his ton of asphalt, he envisioned going home empty that evening, and each and every day he did. His approach was reflected in each and every sales presentation that he made.

Prior to Mr. Phillips' unfortunate death in 1980, he had built Phillips and Sons paving to a forty-man crew with a fleet of a dozen large trucks and lots of support equipment to handle very big projects. I remember in 1978 he mentioned that he was earning $200,000 per year, which by most standards is a lot of money. The nearest that I can figure is that my father had earned about eighteen thousand dollars in his last year of working in 1970. Although there was an eight-year difference in the two years' earnings, there is a huge spread between eighteen thousand dollars and $200,000. Mr. Phillips would be the first to admit that my father was smarter than he, so what does this say for all those smart folks working at secure companies?

DON'T FORGET THE IMPORTANT THINGS

All enterprises of any kind start with an idea, whether it is yours or someone else's.

Any success must have a plan plus a number of contingency plans for each component of the total plan.

You MUST recruit outside opinion from those you respect in the particular field of expertise (your mastermind alliance).

You MUST execute your plan. Taking action is the absolute most important component of the entire process. Without action you are assured of no success.

Positive Thoughts are all you should occupy your mind with.

Visualize your success before you begin, this is an excellent motivator.

Do not let outside opinion rain on your parade unless it is from a multitude of sources you truly respect for their knowledge on the subject. And even then by folding in your contingencies and accounting for variables and change, your respected sources may see hope in your plans.

Remember that one thing everyone in the world has in common with one another, but few would realize, is 24 hours in a day, make the absolute best use of yours.

Remember how powerful the art of pursuasion is, we are all salesmen. Utilize and tap into the heart mind relationship.

Prioritize when planning, since time utilization is so important, learn to recognize and implement your procedure by priority. You can not harvest your crops before the seeds have been planted.

Treat everyone in total fairness and good faith, believe me this will increase your advantage tremendously and you will be respected by all those you value. The circle does return!

NOTES